WAYMARKS

SOUTH TYROL

easy alpine walks

FRANZ HAULEITNER
HENRIETTE KLIER

SUNFLOWER
BOOKS

First published 1988 by Sunflower Books
12 Kendrick Mews, London SW7 3HG, UK

This book is an English translation of
Rund um Meran
Copyright © 1987 by Bergverlag Rudolf Rother
and *Dolomiten für Bergwanderer*
Copyright © 1986 by Bergverlag Rudolf Rother.
All rights reserved.
Authorised translation from the German language editions
published by Sunflower Books.
Copyright © 1988 Sunflower Books.

PUBLISHER'S NOTE ━━━━━━━━━━━━━━━━━━━

Unlike most of the books we publish, we have not
written, mapped out, or checked the walks in this book.
It is a translation from volumes in the first series of
walking books published by Bergverlag Rudolf Rother,
one of Germany's foremost publishers of mountaineering
books and periodicals. While we cannot accept responsi-
bility for the accuracy of the text and maps, we would
be grateful to receive your comments, which we could
pass on to the original publishers.

Note also that this guide is a compilation of walks
taken from *two* books written by different authors; a
slight variation in style and presentation of the walks is
inevitable. Introductions to the two parts of the book
will be found on pages 6 and 7.

We rely on walkers to take along a good supply of
common sense — as well as our guides — when they go
hiking. If a route is not as described in the text, and
your way ahead is not secure, return to the point of
departure. **Do not attempt to complete a walk under
hazardous conditions.** Please read the General information on pages 8—11 and walk *safely*. Respect not only
the beauty, but also the potential dangers of the Alps!

Translation by the staff of Sunflower Books
Photographs by the authors
Walking maps by Richard Blanke (Meran) and Gertrude
and Wilhelm Wagner (Dolomites)
Overview map by Pat Underwood
Printed and bound in the UK by W S Cowell Ltd, Ipswich
E/DH

CONTENTS

3

The South Tyrol is without doubt one of the most picturesque regions in Europe, with its many unspoilt villages, gaily-coloured windowboxes, and friendly, easy-going atmosphere. Visitors experience genuine hospitality here and have a choice between small inexpensive pensions and 4- and 5-star hotels.

The opportunities for walking are superb, but other sports may be enjoyed as well — mountain climbing, skiing in winter *and* in summer, or relaxing holidays with lake bathing or spa treatment in Meran—Merano.

The locally-grown wines are excellent and inexpensive, the markets are brimming over with fruit of every kind, and the food served in the hotels and restaurants is a delicious mixture of Italian and Austrian cuisine.

The South Tyrol has a thriving crafts industry, and you can visit local craftsmen at work in their wood-carving or sculpture workshops. Music, songs and laughter can be heard all over the region. Excursions by car, bus or on foot will take you to romantic castles and scenic viewpoints, many of them illustrated in this book.

Although the South Tyrol is a popular holiday destination, the region has not been over-commercialised and is ready to receive a greater number of English-speaking visitors. In the South Tyrol you can enjoy the best of both worlds — Italian sunshine, wines and fruit, and Austrian friendliness. Excellent facilities are available all year round, and a good number of the walks in this book may be pursued throughout the year as well.

The South Tyrol is easily reached by car, rail or air. Fly to Verona or Innsbruck: from Innsbruck there are direct coach connections on Wednesdays and Saturdays to Bolzano, the Klausen exit on the Brenner highway, or Meran.

—ERNA LOW
British Representative of the *Landesverkehrsamt*
(Official South Tyrol Tourist Office in Bozen—Bolzano)

The walks in the first part of this book radiate from Meran and take in not only the city itself, but a wide surrounding area known as the 'Burggrafenamt' — the former heart of Old Tirol.

This mountain region offers walks in the shadow of the glacier-covered Ötztal Alps, across the jagged ridges of the Passeier and Texel ranges, on the uplands of the Meran Basin, and in the romantic Ulten and Etsch valleys. Whether you walk in the mountains or down on the valley floor, you will enjoy a mild and sunny climate, with relatively cool temperatures in the summer and pleasantly warm spring and autumn days.

Here in the South Tyrol you will find a landscape that retains its original rustic character of Alpine farming country. You will see not only how nature created the landscape of the Alps, but how man, with determination and tenacity, tamed this wild terrain. This agricultural area has been inhabited for thousands of years. On your walks, you will enjoy the contrasting solitude of the high Alpine mountains and the rich green pastures of the 'alms', the stony wastelands and the friendly and inviting alm-huts and hamlets. Even though most farms and upland villages are now joined to the valleys by roads or small lifts, nevertheless the original harmonious character of the landscape remains.

The twenty-five walks around Meran give you only a taste of this almost-paradisial region, blessed with vineyards, palm trees, chestnut-coppices, apple orchards and scores of attractive villages, churches, castles and stately homes.

It is not surprising that the joyful approach to life in the South Tyrol has been created by the meeting of northern and southern climates, languages, cultures, religions, fruits and wines. It has become something unique, which we hope will be preserved for thousands of years to come.

– HENRIETTE KLIER

Many visitors to the South Tyrol would enjoy walking in the Dolomites, but they want a relaxing holiday. They are not mountaineers and would appreciate some suggestions for the best short walks in the area. The second part of this book describes seventeen easy walks in the South Tyrolean Dolomites. (A companion volume, *Waymarks Dolomites*, outlines 42 walks to the south and east of the South Tyrol.)

You may be surprised to learn that the Dolomites offer a wealth of rambling opportunities for the modest walker. At sub-alpine level — between the individual massifs — there are enchantingly beautiful meadowlands and larch tree forests to be explored. You can walk to wild ravines, picturesque valleys, lonely mountain lakes, isolated alm-huts and shelters, superb viewpoints and easily-climbed peaks. Moreover, since many of the routes are accessible by chair lift, you can often indulge in the pleasurable pursuit of 'downhill mountain-climbing'!

All the walks included in this book are fairly easy and follow well-waymarked routes. They are suitable for fit people of all ages, from children to the elderly. The average walking time to cover a route is between two and three hours; the average climb to be mastered at any one stretch is 300m/985ft. Under the heading 'Refreshments en route' you will find listed shelters providing overnight accommodation, but in no case is an overnight stay obligatory: all the walks make comfortable half-day or full-day excursions.

The presentation of each walk follows the same pattern: the ramble is described on two facing pages and illustrated with a photograph and a map. Planning information is given at the start of each walk.

I hope that everyone who uses this guide will spend many joyful hours exploring the South Tyrol's magnificent Dolomites.

– FRANZ HAULEITNER

Using the book

The Contents show you the plan of the book and, together with the map on pages 10–11, give you an overview of the walks. Important information is given at the start of each walk, in 'shorthand' form. A brief description of the route follows; this is illustrated on an accompanying map. A photograph is also included for each excursion — to inspire you in advance!

Grading of the walks

All of the walks in this book are easily tackled by fit people and can be done without any special training. Walking boots are not necessary; stout shoes will suffice. Note, however, that a few of the walks demand sure-footedness and a head for heights. At the start of each walk the total climb (or descent) is given, *in italic type.*

Waymarking

Almost all of the walks are very well waymarked, and the route numbers are referred to in the text and shown on the walking maps.

Dangers

Although all of the walks follow well-made trails and paths, remember that there is *always* a possibility of danger in the mountains — due to storm damage, rockfalls, sudden thunder- or hailstorms, etc. There are also poisonous snakes in some areas.

Walking times

The walking times given at the start of each walk are generous, but they *do not include any stops.*

Best time of year

The months suggested take into account various factors, such as when the ground is free of snow, when the funiculars operate, when the shelters are open, and when the landscape is most lovely.

Clothing and provisions

Be sure to wear stout shoes with good grip. Knee-length socks are advisable. Carry a cardigan, an anorak and some raingear as well. A small rucksack will hold these, as well as some provisions like fruit and chocolate, if you are not packing a lunch. A water flask is mandatory, and it's always a good idea to carry a whistle. You do not need to take any climbing equipment.

Glossary

In order to keep the price of this book as low as possible, the walking maps have been reproduced directly from the original German guide. Most of the information on the maps is self-explanatory and is given in the language used on local signposts (where German and Italian are both in common usage). The glossary below covers all the terms you will find on the maps or in the text. Heights are shown in metres (1 metre = 3.28 feet), but *total climb/descent* is given in feet as well.

German	English	Italian	English
Alm	pastureland	Bàita	bar, shelter
außer	outer	Bivacco (Biv.)	bivouac
Bach	stream	Capanna (Cap.)	hut, shelter
Berg	mountain	Casera (Cas.)	mountain hut
ehem.	formerly	Cima (C.)	summit, peak
Fels	rock	Col	hill
Gasthof (Ghf.)	guesthouse	Cresta	ridge
Gipfel	peak	Croda	cliff, wall
Hütte (Htt.)	hut, shelter	Forcella (Forc.)	saddle
Höhenweg/route	high-level route	Funivia	funicular, lift
ins	to, into	Lago (L.)	lake
Joch	saddle	Malga	mountain hut
Kapelle	chapel	Monte (M.)	mount
Kirche	church	Passo (Pso.)	pass
klein (Kl./kl.)	little	Pian/o	plateau
nach	to	Ponte (Pte.)	bridge
ober	upper	Pra	meadow
Paß	pass	Rifugio (Rif.)	shelter
Sattel	saddle	Rio, Rivo (R.)	river
Scharte	gap, small pass	Sass, Sasso	rock
See	lake, reservoir	Sella	saddle
Seilbahn	funicular	Sentiero	footpath
Sesselbahn	chair lift	Torre(i)	tower(s)
Spitz	peak	Torrente (T.)	stream
Tal	valley	Val, Valle (V.)	valley
verf.	ruined	Via	trail, path
Waalweg	watercourse		
Wald	forest		
Weg	path, trail		
Wssf.	waterfall		
zum	to, towards		

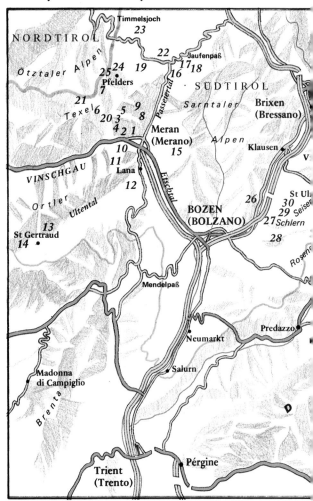

Maps

The map above shows the general location of all
the walks in this book.* Each walk is illustrated
with a large-scale map, so you need not purchase
any special walking maps. However, a good
touring map (suggested scale about 1:200,000)
is essential for getting to the starting point of
any walks located off the main roads shown here.

*A companion volume, *Waymarks Dolomites*, describes 42 addi-
tional walks in the Dolomites to the south and east of South Tyrol.

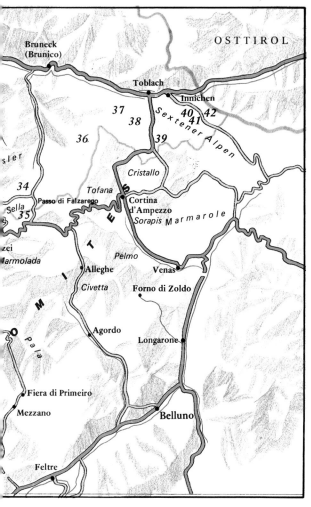

Restaurants, guesthouses, shelters

Most of the restaurants, farms, etc listed under 'Refreshments en route' take overnight guests.

Funiculars and lifts

Several walks in this book start from a point reached by funicular, cabin lift or chair lift. *Do note that many of these operate only in July, August and September.* At other times, the starting point may only be accessible on foot!

Approach: Meran (300m/985ft), an internationally-known health resort, sports and holiday centre at the confluence of the Passeier and Etsch valleys

Starting point/parking: Park in Meran and set out from the parish church at the upper edge of the old city, at the foot of the Segenbühel

Walking time: The Tappeinerweg is 4km long; you can join or leave it anywhere you like. From the Pulverturm to the Café Unterweger *reckon on 1h30min*

Grade: very easy

Highest point: The walk is on level ground, once you have *climbed about 100m/325ft* above Meran.

Best time of year: all year round. Perhaps too hot on sunny summer days, unless you walk in the morning or early evening.

Follow the Tappeinerweg, and you will see all the natural and cultural landscapes of Meran and the vicinity. You'll be captivated by the contrast between the snow-capped mountains above the city and the palms and shrubs in bloom, the rough stone ridges above you and the wealth of grapevines at your feet! Along the way you'll see a plethora of tropical vegetation: palms, oleander, mimosa, different Mediterranean trees and plants, numerous flowers and flowering shrubs. The old city of Meran, dating from the Middle Ages, is visible from the walk, with the attractive tower of the parish church standing out. Far above, Schloß Tirol (Walk 3) and the Brunnenburg will catch your eye — as will the steep peaks of the Zeilspitze in the west.

The Tappeinerweg

From Meran to the Tappeinerweg and the Café Unterweger □
Climb the steps behind St Nicholas Church, and you will come to the Tappeinerweg (which has its start somewhat further east at the Pulverturm*). Follow this asphalted lane in a westerly direction, enjoying the floral display, the very pleasant level walkway, and the ever-changing views over the valley. The ramble ends at the Café Unterweger, where you meet the road from Gratsch to Schloß Thurnstein (bus stop).

Return □ Go back the same way, or take a bus.

Variations (see map page 21) □
Walk on to Schloß Thurnstein and to Dorf Tirol: From the end of the Tappeinerweg, a road leads uphill to Schloß Thurnstein, or you can take a footpath up through the woods (waymarked). From Dorf Tirol a footpath heads down to the old city of Meran, via the Segenbühel hill. □
From the café to the Brunnenburg and on to Schloß Tirol: There is another (steep) footpath from the café to the Brunnenburg and on to to Schloß Tirol. From there you can get a bus back to Meran.

*You can also start the walk here, but the parking is very limited if you come by car.

Approach: Meran (see Walk 1)

Starting point/parking: Dorf Tirol; park at the southern entrance to the village, by the Hotel Gartner.

Refreshments en route: There are numerous restaurants en route.

Walking time: Hotel Gartner—Gratsch 45min; Gratsch—Schloß Thurnstein 40min; Schloß Thurnstein—Dorf Tirol 1h15min; *total time 2h40min.* Variation: Gratsch—Plars—Töll, 3h45min

Grade: an undemanding walk, sometimes on roads

Best time of year: all year round

*T*his walk, which takes you above the Tappeinerweg (Walk 1), makes a circuit of Meran's valley on the northern — sunny — side. For part of the way we follow a 'Waalweg', an irrigation channel or watercourse. On the opposite side of the valley, above Marling, is the longest watercourse in this area — the 12km-long Marlinger Waalweg (Walk 10). Below the watercourses are grapevines, peach and apple trees; above them the slopes are dry and inhospitable.

From the Hotel Gartner in Dorf Tirol to the Algunder Waalweg and back to Dorf Tirol □
Start at the hotel and gently ascend to the left across the slopes of the Küchelberg, following the Schloß Thurnstein road. Above, to the right,

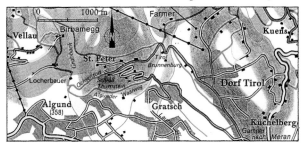

the Brunnenburg stands in a commanding position, on a steep slope planted with apple trees. Schloß Tirol is beyond it. Join the Laurinstraße, and walk up it until you cross the Burgbach. Here leave the Laurinstraße and turn left to join the Waalweg running below the road. This is a particularly lovely stretch of the old watercourse, and you can enjoy magnificent views down onto Gratsch and to Plars in the west. After crossing the Grabbach, another stream, we leave the Waalweg and meet a lane. Head uphill along it, towards the Locherbauer, but branch off right before you reach it, to climb up via the 'Ochsentod Plattenweg' (see also Walk 3) to the Schloß Thurnstein Restaurant. From here return to Dorf Tirol by road, via St Peter.

Variation: From the Waalweg to Töll in the lower Vinschgau (no map) □
After crossing the Grabbach you reach a lane, which is followed to the west for a short time (past the Café Konrad). Then follow the signposted footpath to the Leiter am Waal Restaurant. From there, walk through the vineyards and take the Vinschgau road to Töll. You can return from Töll to Meran by bus.

Opposite: the Algunder Waalweg above Gratsch

Approach: Meran (see Walk 1)

Starting point/parking: Dorf Tirol (640m/2100ft); park at the Tirol parking area at the southern side of the village or at the funicular station.

Refreshments en route: Schloß Tirol, Birbamegg, Schloß Thurnstein restaurants. There are also numerous restaurants in Vellau.

Walking time: from the parking area at the southern side of Dorf Tirol to Schloß Tirol 30min; from Schloß Tirol to Vellau 1h30min; from Vellau back to Dorf Tirol via Schloß Thurnstein about 2h30min; *total time under 5h*

Grade: quite a lot of climbing on narrow, but well-made mountain paths; otherwise good tracks

Highest point: Vellau (900m/2950ft). *Total climb throughout the walk about 350m/1150ft*

Best time of year: possible all year round, but especially lovely in the autumn

---

This circuit on the sunny slopes around Meran visits Schloß Tirol, once the home of the Counts of Tirol; it stands on a moraine west of Dorf Tirol. You'll also see some especially attractive 'Schalenstein' (carved rock) below the path above the Birbamegg Restaurant. The walk affords wonderful views over the Etschtal and to the surrounding mountains.

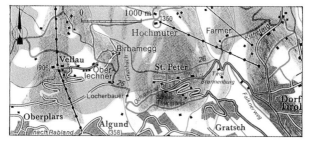

From Dorf Tirol to Vellau via the Birbamegghof □

From the west side of the village (reached via the Falknerweg), you'll see an asphalt lane leading up to Schloß Tirol. Pass it by and cross the Kösten gulley, to come to a fork for Vellau. From here follow Route 26 along the ridge, via St Peter. You will eventually descend to the bed of the Grabbach and then climb up to the Birbamegg Restaurant. From here turn right off the motor road and zig-zag up through the woods, to come to the eastern edge of the meadows outside Vellau. Just another short climb takes you up to Vellau's church.

From Vellau to Dorf Tirol via Schloß Thurnstein □

From Vellau return to the Birbamegghof on the same route. Then take Route 25 and follow the edge of the steep Grabbach gulley down into the valley, finally crossing the stream. Follow the Grabbach down to the Locherbauer Restaurant. Below it, take the path to the left (east), to continue on the 'Ochsentod', an ancient walkway. You will pass a shrine and bench – a pleasant resting place. From here it's a short distance over to the Schloß Thurnstein Restaurant with its viewing terrace. From the restaurant, follow the motor road to the little church of St Peter and back to Schloß Tirol. Then return to Dorf Tirol along your outgoing route.

Schloß Tirol against the backdrop of Ifinger

Approach: Meran (see Walk 1) or Dorf Tirol (640m/2100ft), a holiday centre above Meran

Starting point/parking: Park at the Hochmuter funicular station in Dorf Tirol and take the lift to the Hochmuter Peak (1350m)

Refreshments en route: Hochmuter funicular station; Steinegg, Kienegger, Saxner restaurants; Vellau

Walking time: from the Hochmuter to Vellau 1h15min; from Vellau to the Kienegger Restaurant 45min; from the Kienegger Restaurant to the Saxner Restaurant 1h; from the Saxner Restaurant to Dorf Tirol about 2h; *total time about about 5h*

Grade: The first part of the walk is along a footpath on a somewhat-exposed sheer rock face. It is, however, well-secured with ropes and chains (see photograph). The remainder of the walk follows good tracks and paths.

Highest point: Hochmuter Peak (1350m/4430ft), reached by funicular from Dorf Tirol. *Descent* to Vellau

Best time of year: May to October

This high-level route across the southern slopes above Meran is somewhat lower than the Meraner Höhenweg South (Walk 20). The first part of the walk descends from the Hochmuter Peak to Vellau.

From the Hochmuter mountain station to Vellau □

Take Route 22, a path just above the station. The first part of the way is somewhat exposed, but well protected. The path descends along the western inclines of the mountain, affording wonderful views all round. On crossing the Grabbach, you come into Vellau, by the church.

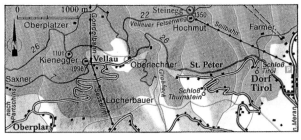

The Vellauer Felsenweg: This is the footpath leading from the Hochmuter to Vellau; waymarking and chain-ropes can be seen to the right.

From Vellau to Dorf Tirol □

In Vellau you meet Route 26, which takes you bach into the Grabbach Valley and via the Birbamegg Restaurant to St Peter and Dorf Tirol.

Variations □

A longer walk takes you from Vellau via the Kienegger Gasthaus to the Saxner Gasthaus and on to Plars and Partschins: From the church in Vellau walk a short distance down to where the way branches. First walk up the road in a westerly direction, then leave it and climb the old walkway up to the Kienegger Restaurant. Pass it and follow Route 26 a bit further, until you meet a fork. Go left here and descend steeply to the Saxner Gasthaus along the Kieneggerweg (labelled '26' on the map). From this restaurant, Route 7 leads you into the Töllgraben.* On the other side of this gulley, descend to Partschins via the houses of Obermaier. □

You can also walk from the Saxner Restaurant to Dorf Tirol via the 'Schlundsteinweg' (Route 25A) and the 'Ochsentod'. See also map page 21.

*This part of the route is not shown on the map.

Approach: Meran (see Walk 1) or Dorf Tirol (see Walk 4)

Starting point/parking: Park at the Hochmuter funicular station in Dorf Tirol and take the funicular to the Hochmuter Peak (1350m)

Refreshments en route: Hochmuter station, Steinegg, Leiteralm, and Birbamegg restaurants; also Vellau

Walking time: from the Hochmuter to the Leiteralm 1h 15min; from the Leiteralm to Vellau 1h15min; from Vellau to Dorf Tirol 1h30min; *total time 5h*

Grade: This footpath has been blasted out of the rock face and is very exposed at some points, but well secured by ropes and chains. The most difficult part is the first 200m (yards) below the Hochmuter Peak (see photograph); beyond this, the paths are less exposed.

Highest point: Leiteralm (1522m/4990ft), reached after a *climb of 172m/565ft*

Best time of year: May until October

Part of the Meraner Höhenweg South (see Walk 20), the beginning of this route is easily reached by funicular from Dorf Tirol. Much of the path has been blasted out of the walls of the Mutspitze; it takes you along rocky inclines high above Meran. You can continue the walk by going further west from the Leiteralm, or return

from there by simply walking back down to the valley. If you follow the walk in the order described here, provided that you start early in the morning, the sun is at your back and you will reach your final destination before it gets too hot. You will have wonderful views all along the way into Meran's valley and to the surrounding mountains.

From the Hochmuter station to the Leiteralm □
From the funicular climb up to the turn-off at the Steinegg Restaurant. Here go left (west) on Route 24 to cross the steep inclines of the Mutspitze with very few 'ups and downs'. You will come to the Leiteralm, a meadowland terrace surrounded by woods.

Descent from the Leiteralm to Vellau and Dorf Tirol □
Follow the footpath (Route 25) down to the church in Vellau. From here Route 26, another excellent footpath, leads you back down to St Peter (via the Birbamegg Restaurant) and across to Dorf Tirol. See also Walks 3 and 4.

Variation □
End the walk at Vellau by taking the two lifts down to Algund, from where you can catch a bus back to Meran.

Opposite: the Hans Frieden Footpath below the Hochmuter station (the most exposed part of the walk)

Approach: Partschins (642m/2105ft), the most easterly village in the lower Vinschgau

Starting point/parking: Park at the station for the (private) Steiner funicular, at the end of the road in the Zielbach Valley (the Birkenwald road). Call for the funicular (there is a telephone), and take it to the Steinerhof.

Overnight lodgings: Lodner Shelter (2259m, 13 beds, 30 bunks, open during the summer). *NB: this is a two-day walk*, and an overnight stay is necessary, unless you are very energetic and prepared to undertake a 9-hour hike! No other refreshments en route

Walking time: from the Steinerhof to the Lodner Shelter about 3h; from the shelter to the lake under 2h; the descent back to the Steinerhof under 4h; *total time — first day (ascent) 3h; second day (ascent and descent) 6h)*

Grade: From the Steinerhof to the Nassereith Shelter (about 20min), the way is narrow and quite exposed; the rest of the walk is on very well-made, ample paths.

Highest point: Halsljoch (2808m/9210ft), reached after a *climb (over two days) of about 1305m/4280ft*

Best time of year: June to September

T aken over two days, this walk is quite easy — one of the few walks in the Texel Group that is accessible to the average hill-walker. This mountain group has become a very popular excursion point since the Birkenwald road was

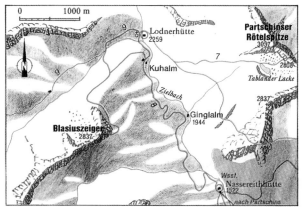

Map note: The Steinerhof is just below the Nassereithhütte.

built. From the Halsljoch, a saddle close by the lake, you will have wonderful views not only to to the Texel Group (we leave its peaks to the mountain-climbers), but also to the Ortler Range.

From the Steinerhof to the Lodner Shelter □
Bear left to follow the narrow footpath to the Nassereith Shelter (signposted). This is the most exposed part of the walk; you must be sure-footed. From here a stone-laid trail (Route 8) takes you to the Lodner Shelter.

From the Lodner Shelter to the lake □
Take Route 7, behind the shelter, and bear right to cross the Zielbach. Bear left at the next fork to cross first grassy, but later rock- and rubble-strewn slopes, and arrive at the basin with the lovely Tabland Lake. From here it's a short hop up to the Halsljoch (labelled '2808' on the map).

The return □ Descend to the Steinerhof and funicular along your outgoing route.

Opposite: Pausing at the Tabland Lake, not far below the Halsljoch. The Blasiuszeiger, a peak you could climb from the Lodner Shelter without too much difficulty, is seen to the left, behind the clouds. The summit in the centre of the photograph is the Gfallwand.

Approach: Pfelders (1662m/5450ft), a village in the heart of the Pfelderertal, 11km from Moos in Passeier

Starting point/parking: Park at the funicular station in Pfelders, and start off from the road at the south side of the village.

Refreshments en route: Zepbichl, Lazins (open all year round), Lazinser Kaser (open in the summer only), Stettinger Hütte (where you can stay overnight, see 'Variation')

Walking time: from Pfelders to the Lazinser Kaser about 1h05min; the return about 1h; *total time just over 2h*

Grade: a very easy walk on country roads and tracks

Highest point: Lazinser Kaser (1868m/6125ft), reached after a *climb of 206m/675ft*

Best time of year: possible all year round, but at its best in the summer months

---

With its unspoilt meadowlands and high, wild slopes, the Pfelderertal is a perfect introduction to South Tyrolean landscapes. The landmark of the area is the 3480m/11,415ft-high peak of the Hochwilde, which marks the western end of the valley. At the southern rim of this peak, at the Eisjöchl, sits the Stettiner Shelter (see 'Variation' opposite).

Looking west from Pfelders, towards Zepbichl and the cloud-covered Hochwilde Peak (3480m/11,415ft)

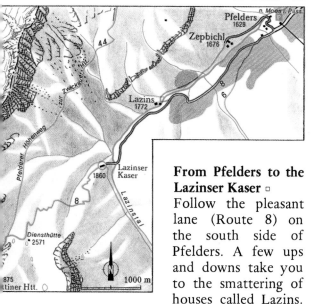

From Pfelders to the Lazinser Kaser □

Follow the pleasant lane (Route 8) on the south side of Pfelders. A few ups and downs take you to the smattering of houses called Lazins. From here the wide lane continues up into the valley to the Lazinser Kaser.

The return □

Go back the way you came, until you return to Lazins. Then cross to the other side of the stream. Now you can wander down a trail, past pastureland huts, to Zepbichl, another hamlet scattered over meadowlands. Not far below, the bridge returns you to your starting point.

Variation (for experienced mountain walkers) □

Beyond the Lazinser Kaser, Route 8 continues to the Stettiner Shelter at the rim of the high plateau. This climb of some 1000m/3280ft takes about 3h. It's easy going at first; then you start to zig-zag steeply uphill. A fork is reached when you attain about 2100m. Here Route 40 heads left (not shown on the map). Bear right to a ruined shelter (Dienshütte). Continue along the southeastern flanks of the Hochwilde to come to the Stettinerhütte (see also references to this shelter in Walks 21 and 25).

Approach: Meran (see Walk 1)

Starting point/parking: Dorf Tirol (640m/2100ft), a holiday centre above Meran. Park on the south side of the village, on the north side (at the Hochmuter funicular), or off the road by the Tiroler Kreuz Restaurant (where the motorable road ends; see 'Hint' below).

Refreshments en route: Dorf Tirol, Ungericht Gasthaus, Tiroler Kreuz Gasthaus, Riffian

Walking time: from Dorf Tirol to Riffian about 2h30min; the return about 1h45min; *total time under 4h*

Grade: quite easy, with no particularly steep ascents

Highest point: Tiroler Kreuz (806m/2645ft), reached after a *climb of about 165m/540ft* (see 'Hint' below)

Best time of year: all year round

Hint: Start at the Tiroler Kreuz, to avoid any climbing.

Whether you enjoy the glorious flowers in spring or feast your eyes on the red and yellow apples and black grapes in autumn, this walk is a delight all year round. Along the route you will see Schloß Auer, a part of the Riffian Waalweg (watercourse), and the pilgrimage church above Riffian (see page 29). Near this church is a cemetery chapel founded in the 8th century by St Korbinian, Bishop of Freising; it contains some interesting frescoes.

From Dorf Tirol to Riffian □

Unless you have parked at the Tiroler Kreuz Restaurant, start in Dorf Tirol. Either walk up the main road to the Tiroler Kreuz, or else take the signposted footpath leading there via the

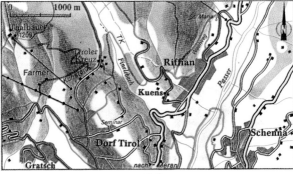

Vineyards above Riffian

seminary. From the Tiroler Kreuz we follow a wide footpath (Route TK) through the forest and into the Finele Valley. At a fork some fifteen minutes along, branch off right to cross the streambed. There is a pretty waterfall here, and a rock pool. On the other side, leave the valley to continue on to the Ungericht Restaurant, reached in about 1h30min from Dorf Tirol. Go right here, and follow the road, making a wide arc down to the gulley above Kuens, where there is a lay-by at Hochübel. Continue on the other side of the gulley down to the Riffian Waalweg, which is followed to the southeast above cultivated terraces and woodlands. This level path leads to a farm above the church of St Maria in Riffian. Take the lane from the farm down to the church. (The Waalweg continues through a forest and on to Saltaus.)

The return □
Go back to Dorf Tirol the same way, or else take a bus from Riffian to Dorf Tirol or Meran. The steps beside the church lead down to the centre of Riffian and the bus stop.

Approach: Kuens (500m/1640ft), a small community to the north of Meran, or Riffian (500m/1640ft), on the Passeier Valley road

Starting point/parking: There is (limited) parking space in the centres of both Kuens and Riffian. Otherwise, you can try the lay-by in the big bend in the road (Hochübel; this is by the bridge at the gulley below the Ungericht Restaurant). There is also parking space at the Ungericht Restaurant.

Refreshments en route: restaurants Ungericht, Bergrast, Walde and Brunner

Walking time: from Kuens or Riffian to the Ungericht Restaurant 35min; from the lay-by at Hochübel to the Ungericht Restaurant 10min; from Ungericht to Gfeis and the Walde Restaurant under 2h; from Gfeis to Vernuer 1h. The descent: from Vernuer to Riffian 2h; from Vernuer to Ungericht (or the lay-by at Hochübel) about 3h; from Gfeis to Riffian about 1h30min. *Total time: depending on the route, approximately 3−5h*

Grade: fairly strenuous, with some steep climbs. The footpaths are very good.

Highest point: Gasthaus Walde (Gfeis, 1296m/4250ft), reached after a *climb of about 796m/2610ft*

Best time of year: May until October

S teep terraces around Gfeis and Vernuer support hamlets that are inhabited all the year round up to an altitude of 1400m. Until a few years ago, these communities could only be reached on foot, but now they are served by a small winding road north of Riffian. Due to its remote location, this area is completely unspoiled and retains its original landscape, architecture and way of life. This enchanting walk is worth the effort!

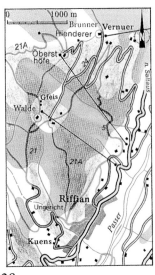

28

St Maria, the pilgrimage church in Riffian (see also Walk 8)

From Kuens or Riffian to Gfeis □

From Kuens, follow the narrow road up past the lay-by on the bend ('Hochübel') and to the Ungericht Gasthaus. From Riffian, start at the southern end of the village (turn off at the Hütterhof) and follow first the road and then a footpath (Route 21): the path leads to the edge of the forest, crosses a watercourse (Waalweg) and then leads left to the road and Restaurant Ungericht. From here we climb up to the Mutlechner Farm and follow Route 21 up through a forest to the Walde Restaurant in Gfeis. (Note that Route 21A leads straight up from Riffian to Gfeis, but our route is not quite as steep.)

From Gfeis to Vernuer □

From the Walde Restaurant follow the lane (Route 24) or the footpath (shown in red) to descend to Vernuer and the Brunner Restaurant.

Descent from Vernuer to Riffian □

From the Gasthaus Brunner a steep tiled track (Route 5, which in bygone days connected the restaurant with the valley) takes us down to Riffian. Alternatively, return the way you came.

Approach: Lana (270m/885ft), 7km southwest of Meran, at the lower end of the Ulten Valley. Due to its mild climate, Lana is the fruit-growing centre for the South Tyrol.

Starting point/parking: Park at the station for the Vigil-joch funicular on the north side of town. The walk starts here.

Refreshments en route: There are numerous restaurants along the route and on the descents into the villages.

Walking times: from Lana to Schloß Vorst, ***total time 2h***

Grade: very easy

Highest point: The watercourse runs about 150m/490ft above the villages of Lana, Tscherms and Marling. The ***only climb is up to the Waalweg from Lana (150m/490ft)***

Best time of year: all year round

The Marlinger Waalweg is the most attractive footpath along the Etsch Valley and affords wonderful views across to Meran and its surrounds. The 12km-long walkway can be approached from several points; equally, you can leave the walk at any time by descending to one of the villages below the watercourse. Even in late autumn the weather tends to be mild, and bright red apples or purple-red grape leaves add colour to the route.

Looking out over Lana to the Laugenspitze (on the right) and the 'nose' of the Gantkofels, from the Marlinger Waalweg

Lana to Schloß Vorst□
Follow the road towards Tscherms for a short stretch, until you see the signpost indicating a left-hand turn up to the Waalweg. Climb up here to the watercourse and turn right onto it (Route 33). Pass a turn-off right down to Tscherms north of the Glögglhof and continue past the Leitenschenke. Further up the slope Lebenberg Castle is in view. Near the Waalheim pass by another descent down to the Etsch. A while later you will come to the Waldschenke. Always continuing on the same contour, you head north until the route bears away to the west (near Schloß

Vorst). Here leave the Waalweg, turning downhill to cross the railway. Then make for the Marling road, via the Lahnweg and the Moserhof. Not far down the valley, by Schloß Vorst, you can catch a bus back to Lana (departures every 20 minutes). Or, if you like, you can walk back into Marling some 3km further on; there is a footpath beside the road.

Approach: Lana (270m/885ft), 7km southwest of Meran and the fruit-growing centre of the South Tyrol

Starting point/parking: Park at the Vigiljoch funicular station on the north side of Lana (near the turn-off of the Ulten Valley road). Take the funicular to the first station (Hotel Vijiljoch, 1486m).

Refreshments en route: Hotel Vijiljoch, Gamplhof, Restaurant Jocher, Seehof, Aschbacherhof

Walking time: from the funicular station to the little church of St Vigil am Joch about 45min; from the church to Aschbach about 35min; from Aschbach to the Seehof about 40min; from the Seehof to the Hotel Vijiljoch 1h; *total time for the entire route under 3h*

Grade: easy walking trails, mostly through woodlands

Highest point: St Vigil Church (1795m/5890ft), reached after a *climb of 309m/1015ft*

Best time of year: May to October

Hint: You can avoid climbing by taking the chair lift from the Hotel Vijiljoch to the summit of the Larchbühel. From there it's a ten-minute descent to St Vigil.

The Vijiljoch is the highest point on the majestic range of mountains to the northwest of Lana. Covered by forests, this range fans out into a massive ridge towering over the northern side of the Ulten Valley. High up on the slopes stands the picturesque little church of St Vigil; it used to mark the border of the

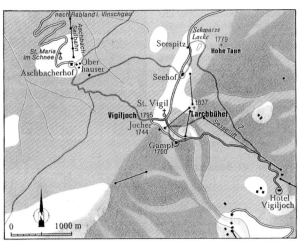

The little church of St Vijil am Joch

bishoprics of Trient and Chur — and no doubt was built to mark this boundary visibly. The walk described here offers fantastic and far-reaching views and can be extremely easy — if you take the chair lift up to the highest point and then treat yourself to some 'downhill mountain walking'.

Circular walk Hotel Vijiljoch—Aschbacherhof—Seehof—Hotel Vijiljoch □

Either follow the road from the top end of the funicular to the Jocher Restaurant and St Vigil, or else (to avoid the 45-minute climb) go there by chair lift. From the church, head back west to the fork, where Route 28 branches off northwest to Aschbach. Follow this trail to descend gently to Aschbach and its mountain station (this funicular comes up from Rabland in the Vinschgau). Nearby is the little church of St Maria im Schnee. A short walk takes us back to the Seehof turn-off. Bear left to follow the path up to the Seehof Restaurant and from there go left on the track to the Schwarze Lacke, a silted-up lake. From the lake follow the footpath (Route 7) back towards the Larchbühel. A short climb up its eastern flanks leads to the wide track that takes us back to the top end of the funicular station, by the Hotel Vijiljoch.

Approach: Völlan (718m/2355ft), a popular holiday centre in the northern part of the Tisens uplands

Starting point/parking: There is nowhere to park in the village, so find some space on the outskirts. The walk starts on the edge of Völlan, near the farming museum; this is easily reached from the village centre.

Refreshments en route: numerous restaurants in Völlan; also the Talmühle and Plattner restaurants

Walking time: from Völlan to the Talmühle and St Hippolyth about 45min; from St Hippolyth to Völlan about 45min; *total time 1h30min.* (See also 'Variations' on the next page.)

Grade: an easy stroll with a few ups and downs

Highest point: St Hippolyth (758m/2485ft); the walk is only steep for this short ascent to the church

Best time of year: all year round

Hint: There are some variations of this walk — see opposite.

Set on a rocky hillock above the Etsch Valley, the little church of St Hippolyth has long been revered as a holy place. Many prehistoric finds confirm that the area around Völlan was settled very early on, probably because of its sheltered position and easy access.

From Völlan to St Hippolyth Church via the Talmühle Restaurant

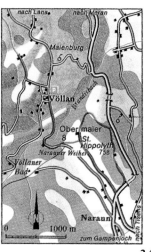

('Mill in the Valley') □ From the edge of Völlan (Widum, farming museum), take the lane (Route 8) down into the bed of the Brandisbach and carry on to the 'Talmühle' (the 'mill in the valley'). You cross the stream and walk up through a forest on the other side. The ground levels out, and a wonderful landscape

St Hippolyth atop its hillock

of meadows with ancient chestnut trees surrounds you. A farm is passed on your right, and
then you descend into a little valley. A forest
footpath and finally an ancient walkway hewn
from rock takes you up to the wonderfully-sited
church shown above.*

The return □ Follow the same route back.

Variations □
If you have time, you might like to circle the
hillock before returning to Völlan. Start by
following the lane leading southwest from the
church down to the Gampenjoch road. Bear
right on it and follow it to the first little lane
on your right. Turn right and carry on to the
Obermaier Farm. Having rounded the hillock,
you now meet your ascending path again; follow
your outgoing route down to the mill in the
valley and back to Völlan. Add about 30 minutes for this circuit. □
Alternatively, if you haven't much time, you can
walk to St Hippolyth from the Gampenjoch
road. Coming from Meran to the Gampenjoch,
park at the lay-by just beyond the second tunnel.
From here it's a 15-minute climb up to the
church.

*Publisher's note: The symbol for St Hippolyth is missing from
the map; it should be to the right of '758' (where there is a ■).

Approach: St Gertraud (1400m/4590ft), or St Nikolaus (1250m/4100ft), both in the meadowland heart of the Ulten Valley

Starting point/parking: Restaurant Edelweiß on the main road to St Gertraud

Refreshments en route: ample restaurants in St Gertraud and St Nikolaus

Walking time: from St Gertraud to Urlärchen and St Nikolaus about 1h20min; the return about 1h30min; *total time under 3h*

Grade: an undemanding walk with a few ups and downs; all on good trails and country roads

Highest point: The walk is always in the valley, and the route *undulates between 1200–1500m (3935–4920ft).*

Best time of year: all year round

A visit to the heart of the Ulten Valley takes you back to the original landscape and character of the South Tyrol and its villages. Beyond St Nikolaus the majority of the settlement is rural. Archaeological finds show that this area has been inhabited for a very long time; however, its inaccessibility means that it has not long been on the 'tourist circuit'. Often, the valley has been a place of hiding or of refuge.

From St Gertraud to St Nikolaus □
The road into the centre of St Gertraud branches off near the Gasthaus Edelweiß, where you can

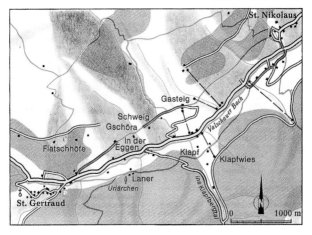

park. Before setting off for St Nikolaus, walk up to St Gertraud's church. From the adjacent cemetery, there are some very fine views of the area. Then take the trail from the car park to St Nikolaus. This leads you along the right-hand side of the valley, through meadowland and past the Laner Farm. Above it, in the forest, are some wonderful old larch trees (Urlärchen on the map). Three of them are reputed to be 2000 years old, and one has a trunk with a circumference of 8m (26ft)! Somewhat further along, you cross the forestry road leading down into the Klapfberg Valley. Climbing out of this gulley, continue to St Nikolaus.

From St Nikolaus to St Gertraud □
Set off from the northern end of the village, by the parish church. Here you will find a sign-posted trail to St Gertraud; it passes the St Nepomuk Chapel and continues along the sunny slopes. When you reach the Gasteig Farm, you pick up the main valley road and follow it to the car park, via the farms of Schweig and Eggen.

Opposite: mountain farmsteads on the 'Sonnenhang' – the 'sunny slopes' of the Ulten Valley

Approach: St Gertraud (1400m/4590ft), in the heart of the Ulten Valley

Starting point/parking: Weißbrunner See, a reservoir at 1900m/6230ft. At the Edelweiß Restaurant outside St Gertraud, the main road bears left into the village. Here go *straight ahead* up to the reservoir. This road is narrow in places, but well-surfaced. Park at the reservoir.

Refreshments en route: at Weißbrunn; also at the Höchster Hütte (shelter)

Walking time: from the reservoir to the Höchster Shelter about 1h30min; from the shelter to the reservoir via the Langsee and Fischer See about 3h; *total time 4h30min*

Grade: a fairly strenuous, but very popular and well-waymarked walking route; the paths are very good.

Highest point: Höchster Shelter (2561m/8400ft), reached after a *climb of 689m/2260ft*

Best time of year: May until early October

Due to the fairly new road up to the Weißbrunner See, a reservoir, this area in the upper Ulten Valley has become very popular with walkers. The drive up past the last mounside farmsteads takes you by some very steep slopes. From the Höchster Hütte (the 'highest shelter'), you look out across to the glaciers of the Zufrittspitze and the two Eggen peaks. Below you lies another shimmering green reservoir, the Grünsee. After the Second World War, five large electricity-generating plants were built in the Ulten Valley, hence the lovely reservoirs. Apart from the loss of valuable arable

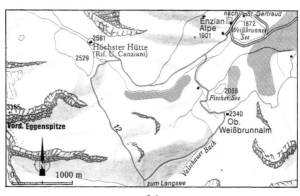

Above the Weißbrunner See, one of the reservoirs in the upper Ulten Valley

land (many farms were flooded), the project has been generally beneficial to the economy of the valley.

From the Weißbrunner See to the Höchster Hütte □

Take the good trail that begins on the western side of the reservoir. It takes you through a forest and then over open ground up to the new 'Highest Shelter', above the Grünsee. (The original shelter was flooded when they built the reservoir.)

From the shelter to the Weißbrunner See, via the other reservoirs □

Begin by following the trail (Route 12) downhill from the shelter, then turn off right, to the top of the reservoir walls. Cross them and, on the other side, continue via the slopes of the Eggenspitze down to the Langsee. Here's the source of the 'wild' Valschauer Stream that flows down the Ulten Valley and into the Etsch by Lana. The continuation of our trail heads left in a northeasterly direction *before* we reach the Langsee; go back to the fork and bear right to continue via the uplands of the Weißbrunner Alm to the Fischer See. (From here a footpath descends directly into St Gertraud.) We leave this reservoir and descend through a lovely pine forest back to our outgoing route, where we bear right to return to the Weißbrunner See.

Approach: Meran (see Walk 1)

Starting point/parking: Hafling Dorf (1300m/4265ft), a village southeast of Meran on the extensive high plateau above the Etsch Valley. This area is commonly referred to as the 'Tschögglberg'. Approach from Meran and park beyond the tunnel.

Refreshments en route: Gasthaus Brunner, Leadner Alm, Wurzer Alm, Vöraner Alm

Walking time: from the parking place to the Wurzer Alm about 1h; from the Wurzer Alm to the Vöraner Alm about 1h; from the Vöraner Alm to Hafling about 1h 45min; *total time about 3h45min*

Grade: a fairly strenuous walk, but the paths and trails are excellent and the waymarking good

Highest point: Vöraner Joch, a saddle at 1932m/6335ft, reached after a *climb of about 630m/2070ft*

Best time of year: May until October

The Hafling high plateau is undulating and cloaked in forests and meadowlands. This area offers a variety of landscapes and rises from 1200m to 2000m. Surrounded by steep cliffs, it can only be approached via a few roads — or on foot. Due to its altitude, the plateau is a lovely place for fairly energetic and refreshing walks.

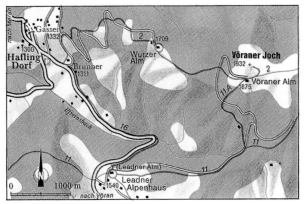

From Hafling to the Vöraner Joch □
Climb from the car park up to the Brunner Restaurant. From here follow the road for a short time; then take Route 2. A gentle ascent, mainly through a forest, takes you to the Wurzer Alm. From this pastureland shelter continue to the Vöraner Alm. Now it's just a short climb up to the saddle (the Vöraner Joch), from where there are unimpeded views to the east, into the Sarn Valley.

From the Vöraner Joch to Hafling □
Return from the saddle to the Vöraner Alm. From here Routes 11a and 11 take you through the forest to the Leadner Alm. A lane (Route 16) carries you from here back to Hafling. Just beyond the Leadner Alm, you can cut the first loop off the road by taking a footpath (not shown on the map, but waymarked Route 16).

Opposite: the Hafling Plateau, a walkers' paradise. Hafling horses originate from this area and are still bred on these colourful meadowlands.

Approach: St Martin (600m/1965ft), the largest settlement in the Passeier Valley, with an old town centre and numerous new buildings

Starting point/parking: Park in the village of St Martin or on any suitable point off the Prantach road. The walk starts near the bus stop at the southern exit to St Martin, on the Prantach road.

Refreshments en route: Pfandlerhof, Pfandleralm

Walking time: ascent from the valley to the Pfandleralm between 2h–2h30min; descent about 2h; *total time under 4h30min*

Grade: a fairly easy ascent if you follow the road; otherwise a steeper ascent via signposted footpaths

Highest point: Pfandleralm (1350m/4430ft), reached after a *climb of 750m/2460ft*

Best time of year: early spring until October

Hint: You can drive from St Martin along the Prantach road, to a point where you would have a climb of only 30 minutes to the Pfandleralm.

Above St Martin to the east lies the village of Prantach, a settlement of widely-scattered houses reaching up to about 1200m. A narrow asphalt road curls up to Prantach and beyond it, to the Pfandlerhof (only farmed during the summer months). Some 2km north

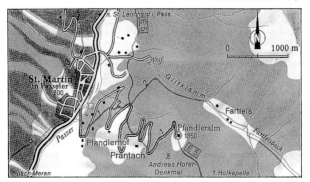

of St Martin, on the road, is the Sandhof — the birthplace of Andreas Hofer, a famous free-dom-fighter. The Pfandleralm was his last place of refuge; he was arrested there in 1810.

From St Martin to the Pfandleralm □

Follow the Prantach road, leaving St Martin from the southeast. Cross the bridge over the Passer (Johannesbrücke) and round the mountainside. If you wish to use the footpath (Route 1), this short-cut is shown on the map: it leads uphill across meadows and through a small wood, crossing the road several times. Either route takes us past the old castle chapel above on our right and the Gruber Farm (dating from the Middle Ages), before we come to the Pfandler-hof. From here a broad meadowland trail continues to the Pfandleralm, surrounded by woodlands. At the edge of the meadow is a memorial to Andreas Hofer.

The return □

Follow the same route back. You may notice, when you return to the castle chapel, footpaths branching off to either St Leonhard (Route 5) or the Fartleiseralm (Route 2). Then, shortly before you return to the Johannesbrücke, a meadowland footpath on the left (Route 5) leads to Saltaus.

Opposite: the old farm chapel below the Gruberhof

Approach: Innerwalten (1450m/4755ft), a little village 13km from St Leonhard, on the Jaufen Pass road

Starting point/parking: Wanns (1420m). Wanns is reached via a narrow unsurfaced road from Innerwalten. The turn-off is signposted 'Tirolerheim'. Park at the Wannser Hof (beyond which the road is no longer motorable).

Refreshments en route: Wannser Hof, Wannser Alm, Seebergalm

Walking time: from St Johann via the Jägersteig to the Wannser Alm and Seeberg Lake, then back to St Johann, *total time about 3h30min*

Grade: a straightforward climb along wide trails or well-signposted footpaths

Highest point: flanks of the Seebergspitze (about 1850m/6070ft), reached after a *climb of about 420m/1380ft*

Best time of year: May until the end of October

'**J**ägersteig' means 'hunters' footpath', and this path takes us through a forest up and around the wide rim of the Seeberg Lake. We begin by climbing the ridge between the Wannser and Sailer valleys, up to the Wannser Alm.

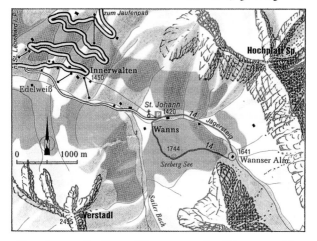

Circular walk from Wanns to the Wannser Alm (Jägersteig) and Seeberg Lake, then back to Wanns □

From the Wannser Hof take the wide meadow-land track (Route 14). You will first pass the Gschloßalm hut. The track climbs steeply at first and then evens out to continue deeper into the valley. The Wannser Alm lies on a slope to the right. Here you will find a signpost, 'Jäger-steig'. The path zig-zags up* through a thick forest towards the flanks of the Seebergspitze (see also Walk 18 and map page 47). This walk parts company with Walk 18 well below the Wannser Joch, and we descend to the Seeberg Lake and nearby Seebergalm. Below the See-bergalm, a good trail zig-zags down the right-hand side of the Sailer Stream through woods. In the lower Sailer Valley leave the trail, to take the footpath branching off right and descend steeply to the Wannser Hof.

*See also map page 47, which shows the Seebergspitze. The route of Walk 17 shown in red above does not include the climb above the Wannser Alm. Reckon on climbing about 200m above the Wannser Alm, before descending to the Seeberg Lake.

Opposite: the little church of St Johann in Wanns. See also photograph for Walk 18.

Approach: Innerwalten (1450m/4755ft), a little village 13km from St Leonhard, on the Jaufen Pass road

Starting point/parking: Wanns (1420m). Wanns is reached via a narrow unsurfaced road from Innerwalten. The turn-off is signposted 'Tirolerheim'. Park at the Wannser Hof (beyond which the road is no longer motorable)

Refreshments en route: Wannser Hof, Wannser Alm, Seebergalm

Walking time: from the Wannser Hof to Wannser Joch about 2h; from the Wannser Joch to the Alpspitze about 20min; descent from the peaks to Wanns about 2h15min; *total time about 5h*

Grade: Most of the climb is along good tracks and well-made paths. However, from the Wannser Joch to the Sailerjoch the (unwaymarked) path is quite exposed. You must be sure-footed and have a head for heights. Otherwise, go back to the fork and descend as Walk 17.

Highest point: Alpspitze (2477m/8125ft), reached after a *climb of 1057m/3465ft*

Best time of year: June until the end of September

This is a walk for the energetic who are sure-footed and have a head for heights! Your reward will be a plunging view straight down more than 1000m/3280ft into the Sarntal from the Wannser Joch. You climb to this saddle on an old military 'road'; even if you have no head for heights, you *could* still tackle this climb and return the way you came, or via the Seeberg Lake (see Walk 17). It's only beyond the Wannser Joch that the footpath is exposed.

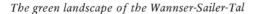

The green landscape of the Wannser-Sailer-Tal

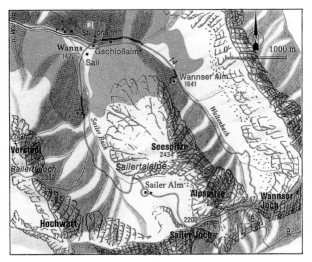

From the Wannser Hof to the Alpspitze □

Take Route 14, a wide trail. At first the ascent is steep (along the Jägersteig; we share this route with Walk 17). Then it levels out as you approach the Wannser Alm. From here continue along the signposted footpath towards the inner valley and finally zig-zag up left to the Wannser Joch, where there is a cross. From this pass a good small footpath takes you to the top of the Alpspitze.

From the Wannser Joch to the Sailer Joch □

Return from the Alpspitze to the Wannser Joch, then take the narrow footpath on the Sarn Valley side of the pass, to cross steep grassy slopes and reach the Sailer Joch.

From the Sailer Joch down to Wanns □

Descend the slopes in a westerly direction. You reach a marshy high plateau, which has to be crossed. When you come to the remains of a wall on the top of a little hillock, follow the wall to the right and continue down to the Sailer Alm beside a little stream. Near the pastureland, cross the stream and descend into the valley. You leave the valley on the left side. Before reaching the Sailer Hof, walk over to the right and cross the stream; then continue to the Wannser Hof.

Approach: Moos in Passier (1007m/3300ft), at the confluence of the Passeiertal and the valley leading to Pfelders

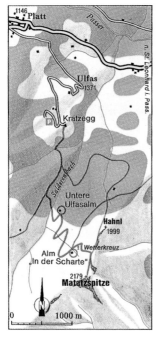

Starting point/parking: Kratzegg (1400m), on the road to Platt, some 2.6km beyond Moos. Beyond Platt, turn off the Pfelders road and bear left for Ulfas (signpost); continue beyond Ulfas to Kratzegg, the highest farm. There is a car park at the end of the motorable stretch of road.

Refreshments en route: Untere Ulfasalm, Alm 'In der Scharte'

Walking time: from Kratzegg up to the peak about 2h15min; the descent about 2h; *total time about 4h15min*

Grade: an undemanding climb on good trails as far as the Alm 'In der Scharte' (first hour). Beyond this pastureland, paths are steep and stony. Some scree must be crossed before reaching the summit. If you are climbing to the Hahnl and Matatzspitze, you must be sure-footed and have a head for heights. Otherwise, go only as far as the Alm 'In der Scharte'.

Highest point: Matatzspitze (2179m/7145ft), reached after a *climb of 700m/2295ft*

Best time of year: June until the end of September

For those with energy, the hike described here leads to three wonderful viewpoints: the Wetterkreuz, the Hahnl, and the Matatzspitze. These high points all rise from the majestic ridge which begins in the heart of the Texel Group and extends downwards via the Kilbenspitze (2868m), the Muthspitze (2246m) and the Matatzspitze to the meadowland terraces of Christl and Pircha southwest of St Leonhard.

From these vantage points, you will overlook the upper Passeier Valley in the north, as well as St Martin in Passeier and the Sarntal Alps rising in the east.

From the Kratzegg Farm to the Alm 'In der Scharte' and the Wetterkreuz and Hahnl □

Follow the road from the car park below Kratzegg, to pass the old mill and return to the farm buildings. From here head into the forest and continue towards the valley along the lane. It carries you to the meadows of the Untere Ulfasalm and curves round the pastureland huts. From here continue on the path which begins outside the cattle fence on the upper edge of the pastures and leads uphill through a light wood. Above the Ulfasalm a path branches off to the south, to round the Matatzspitze and continue to the Muthspitze. We head *north*, left, and come to the little hut 'In der Scharte', with a pleasant open-air resting place. From here keep left to zig-zag up the wide ridge to the Wetterkreuz and Hahnl.

Ascent of the Matatzspitze □

After climbing the Hahnl, just follow the ridge to the summit of the Matatzspitze.

The return □

You can descend directly from the Matatzspitze to the Alm 'In der Scharte'; then follow your outgoing route.

Farms at Außerhütt, at the foot of the Matatzspitze

Approach: Katharinaberg in the west; St Leonhard in the east

Starting points/parking: You can start at several points. By car you can drive to (from west to east): Katharinaberg, Staud, Gfeis (Restaurant Walde or Restaurant Bergrast), Vernuer, Magdfeld, Matatz, Ulfas, Kratzegg, or Pfelders. The walk can be joined from these villages. Perhaps the easiest way to start is by parking in Dorf Tirol and taking the funicular to the Hochmuter Peak. Other funiculars or lifts: Kopfron (east of Katharinaberg), Unterstell (below Lint), Hochforch, Gigglberg, Steinerhof, Leiteralm

Refreshments en route/overnight suggestions: Almost all the farms en route offer refreshments and a bed for the night. There are numerous restaurants and guesthouses.

Walking times: Hof Unterpferl in Katharinaberg–Dickhof 1h30min; Dickhof–Gruber 1h20min; Gruber–Hochforch 2h; Hochforch–Gigglberg 1h; Gigglberg–Nassereith 1h15min; Nassereith–Tablander Alm 1h 15min; Tablander Alm–Hochganghaus 2h; Hochganghaus–Leiteralm 1h30min; Leiteralm–Hochmuter funicular station 1h15min; Hochmuter–Talbauer 40min; Talbauer–Longfall 1h30min; Longfall–Gfeis 1h30min; Gfeis–Vernuer 1h; Vernuer–Magdfeld 1h30min; Magdfeld–Matatz 2h; Matatz–Kristl 1h; Kristl–Ulfas 1h30min; *total time about 24h*

Grade: very stout shoes, lots of energy, sure-footedness and a head for heights are absolutely essential! The well-signposted footpath (Route 24) is very good.

Highest point: the route undulates between 100 and 1500 metres, with each stretch involving some ascents and descents

Best time of year: May to early November

This high-level walk can be particularly recommended to those who do not like steep ascents and descents. You can 'dip into' the walk wherever you like, depending on your preferences, mood and how fit you are! At several points you can climb to a summit . . . or not. Nor need you follow a rigid timetable. The walking times given above simply give you an indication of distances. Apart from the magnificent views into the valleys and across the mountains, you will also pass a number of very attractive farms, scattered over steep inclines. Until a few

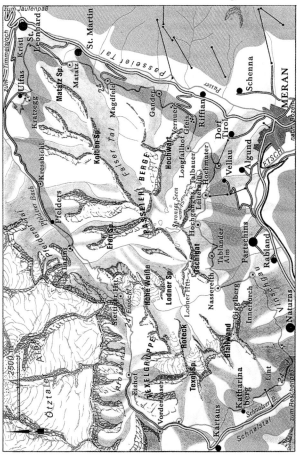

years ago, when roads and cable-cars opened up
the area, these farms were isolated and almost
completely cut off from the valleys. The walk
takes you along the 'Vinschgauer Sonnenberg',
the sunny side of the slopes. Unlike the northern
part of the Meraner Höhenweg, the route is
passable well into the autumn. And whereas the
northern 'Highroad' passes through valleys
abounding in streams, this route crosses steep
arid slopes. All attempts to establish trees here
seem to have failed. But by their persistence —
not to say stubbornness — the farmers have
nevertheless created a little paradise.

Approach from the west: Naturns (594m/1950ft); from here drive up to Katharinaberg (1245m) high above the Schanls Valley.

Approach from the east: Moos in Passeier (see Walk 19).

Starting points/parking: If approaching from the west, park at Katharinaberg and start from the Montfert Farm 226m above the village. From the east, park at Kratzegg (see Walk 19).

Refreshments en route/overnight suggestions: There are several guesthouses in Katharinaberg and Pfelders. Also: Jägerrast, Vorderkaser, Mitterkaser, Eishof, Stettiner Hütte, Lazinser Alm, Lazins (open all year round), Zepbichl, Innerhütt, Ulfas, Kristl, Matatz

Walking time: *For the entire route reckon on 16 hours.* Katharinaberg—Montfert—Eishof 3h30min—4h; Eishof—Stettiner Shelter 3h30min; Stettiner Shelter—Pfelders 3h30min; Pfelders—Ulfas—Matatz 5h. **Map page 51**

Grade: The path (Route 24) presents no difficulties — as there is no snow. However, you must be very fit, surefooted and used to heights. The crossing over the Eisjöchl is very demanding. While the southern stretch of the Meraner Höhenweg is passable from May to November, this northern part leads up to much higher altitudes. Information about conditions around the Eisjöchl can be obtained from the tourist centres in Schnals (tel: 89148) or Moos (tel: 85558).

Highest points: Vorderkaser in the Pfosental (1693m), Stettinger Shelter (2875m), Lazinser Kaser (1868m), Pfelders (1662m). *Steepest climb en route: 800m/2625ft*

Best time of year: late June to early September

Having described the southern stretch of the Meraner Höhenweg, it would be a pity to omit the northern part of the walk. However, do bear in mind that this is far more strenuous and does not permit short 'hops' from

Above Katharinaberg, with views to the Ötztal Ridge

The Steinegg Guesthouse (Meraner Höhenweg South)

one village to the next, as does Walk 20. This part of the 'Meran Highroad' is only recommended for experienced mountain hikers.

From Katharinaberg to Pfelders □
Climb up from the village to Montfert, a little group of houses. High above the confluence of the Schnals and the Pfossenbach, you climb to the floor of the Pfossen Valley. The route leads past the Vorderkaser and the Mitterkaser to the Eishof. From here continue along the valley floor, then bear left towards the slopes. Cross two streams before zig-zagging up to the Eisjöchl and then quickly down to the Stettiner Shelter. This stretch involves a climb of some 800m/2625ft. The route from here to Pfelders is described in Walk 7 under 'Variations'.

From Pfelders to Ulfas □
From Pfelders follow the main valley road for a short time. At Außerhütt (photo page 49) our route leaves the road and takes us up to Ulfas (1370m, above Platt). From Ulfas climb up to the car park at the Kratzegg Farm. (Or take a bus direct from Pfelders to Moos or St Leonhard.)

Approach: St Leonhard (688m/2255ft), 24km below the Timmelsjoch, at the confluence of the Passer and Walten streams

Starting point/parking: Park at the 'Glaiten bend' on the Jaufen Pass road (6km above St Leonhard). There is a kiosk here and bus connection to St Leonhard. The walk starts at the car park.

Refreshments en route: several restaurants in Glaiten and Stuls; also the kiosk at the Glaiten bend in the road

Walking time: from the 'Glaiten bend' (kiosk) to Glaiten 20min; Glaiten to Stuls 1h15min; the return about 15min; *total time under 3h*

Grade: an easy walk on well-signposted trails

Highest point: Stuls (1315m/4315ft), reached after a *climb of about 100m/325ft*

Best time of year: all year round

Hint: Some interesting variations are possible, if you travel by bus and do not have to return to your car at the Glaiten bend in the road. See 'Variations'.

Here's an excursion to the sunniest parishes of the Passeier Valley. The route is almost level walking — at a height of about 1200-1300 metres — through meadows and woodlands. Some of the lovely views are shown in the photograph opposite.

From the 'Glaiten bend' on the Jaufen Pass road to Glaiten and Stuls □

Start at the kiosk and follow the broad track west. Climb up to see the little church of St Hippolyth. Return to the track and continue

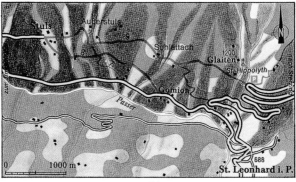

Looking west from Stuls towards the Ötztal Range

on Route 9, passing the farms of Glaiten and Schlattach. From there continue through a forest and over meadowlands. Below a chapel on the eastern outskirts of Stuls, we enjoy very fine views from a rocky knoll (where there are also the remains of a significant prehistoric settlement). A streambed is crossed before we reach the centre. Some particularly attractive old farmhouses adorn the sunny slopes above Stuls.

The return □ If you left your car on the Jaufen Pass road, go back the way you came.

Variations □

From Stuls you can take a bus back to St Leonhard. □

From Stuls you can take Routes 8 and 7 down to Gomion on the Timmelsjoch road, and from there walk back to St Leonhard (under 2h). □

From Stuls you can also walk to Moos in Passier (not shown on the map): In the village, go west and down to the Wiesenhof. From there carry on to the Schöphof, through a forest. Continue down the steep slopes (Sattelhöfe) until you come to concrete steps; these lead down to the road. Follow the road up the valley, through tunnels. An impressive waterfall lies en route!

Approach: St Leonhard (688m/2255ft), 24km below the Timmelsjoch, at the confluence of the Passer and Walten streams

Starting point/parking: Saltnuss (1680m), on the Timmelsjoch road (15km from St Leonard or 7km from Moos). Park near the track where the walk starts: this is just east of Saltnuss, on the western side of the Schneeberg Stream

Refreshments en route: Schneeberg Shelter, run by the Alpine Club and open in the summer only (2355m)

Walking time: from the parking place to the Schneeberg Shelter 2h; the descent about 1h45min; *total time under 4h*

Grade: a straightforward climb on an old military route

Highest point: Schneeberg Shelter (2355m/7725ft), reached after a *climb of 675m/2215ft*

Best time of year: June to the end of September

Hint: From the Schneeberg Shelter you can follow a good footpath to the Schwarzsee, a lake at 2609m/8555ft. Allow an hour to climb there and 45min to return.

Long past are the days when thousands of miners worked at St Martin am Schneeberg — the highest mine in Europe. This easy hike takes us through a magnificent larch forest and over lovely alpine pastures to the 'ghost town' of the derelict mining settlement . . . and perhaps on to the solitude of the Schwarzsee.

From the car park to the Schneeberg Shelter ▫
Our footpath begins at the little lay-by on the Timmelsjoch road, approximately 200m (yards) uphill from the bridge crossing the Schneeberg

Stream'. There is a signpost for St Martin here. Go straight through the forest, ascending quite steeply, first in a northerly and then a north-easterly direction. You pass the large crucifix mounted on a rock — the 'Christus am Feuer-kofel'. Follow the wide trail through the light wood and then come to an open area, from where there are particularly good views down to the right (south). Beyond the Schneeberg Stream, in the direction of the Saltnuss pas-turelands, the slag-heaps of the old Kaindlstollen (opened in 1660) are visible. Climb the slope up to a gulley, where peat was cut in the past. Finally, make a wide arc up to the Schneeberg Shelter, surrounded by the ruins of the old mining 'town'. From here you can follow a good trail — almost level walking — towards the valley floor (northeast). Here, a fairly steep foot-path climbs up the grassy slope. You'll pass a silted-up lake and climb over a boulder- and scree-strewn ridge to get up to the Schwarzsee ('Black Lake'), set deep in a gulley and sur-rounded by rocks and scree.

The return □ Follow the same route back.

Opposite: some of the ruins at St Martin am Schneeberg

Approach: Pfelders (1662m/5450ft), in the heart of the Pfelderertal, 11km from Moos in Passeier

Starting point/parking: Park at the entrance to Pfelders and start out from the bridge by the Edelweiß Restaurant (at the northern exit from the village).

Refreshments en route: Pfelders, Oberstein

Walking time: from Pfelders to Oberstein 35min; from Oberstein to Imstalm about 1h30min; the descent about 1h30min; *total time just over 3h30min*

Grade: very easy to Oberstein. The path to Imstalm is not recommended for inexperienced walkers. It is very steep and exposed (though secured by chains).

Highest point: Imstalm (2214m/7260ft), reached after a *climb of 586m/1920ft*. Otherwise, there is hardly any ascent to Oberstein.

Best time of year: to Oberstein — all year round; to Imstalm — June to September

---

The relatively new road to Pfelders allows quick and easy access to the villages on the northern side of the Pfelderertal. Today's casual holiday-maker can hardly imagine how desolate and dangerous this area was before the road was built.

From Pfelders to Oberstein □
Beginning at the bridge by the Edelweiß Restaurant, keep right and follow the meadowland track to leave the valley. The farms of a hamlet, Unterstein, are to your right. A short climb on a

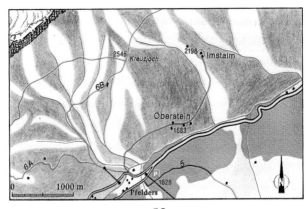

The meadow slopes below Oberstein

wide track takes you up into Oberstein. This
little grouping of farms still retains its original
buildings, including the baking oven tucked
beneath rock. You'll find the old mill where the
stream cascades over the steep edge of the
meadow.

From Oberstein to the Imstalm □
The footpath, which climbs steeply over rough
and rocky terrain, starts just behind the restaurant ('In der Schran'). Crossing steep grassy
slopes, you walk up to the pastureland with its
little hut.

Approach: Pfelders (1662m/5450ft), in the heart of the Pfelderertal, 11km from Moos in Passeier

Starting point/parking: Park at the entrance to Pfelders (car park) and start out from the bridge by the Edelweiß Restaurant (at the northern exit from the village).

Refreshments en route: Untere Schneidalm, Pfelders; also Zwickauer Shelter (see 'Hint' below)

Walking time: from Pfelders to the Untere Scheidalm about 1h45min; the descent about 1h30min; *total time just over 3h15min*

Grade: a fairly steep climb on a well-made footpath

Highest point: Untere Schneidalm (2170m/7115ft), reached after a *climb of 542m/1775ft*

Best time of year: June to October

Hint: Experienced mountain hikers might like to continue from the Untere Schneidalm to the Zwickauer Shelter (open in the summer only). This path is not easy; you must be sure-footed and have a head for heights. The Zwickauer Shelter lies above the permanent snowline. See 'Variation' opposite.

The views into the valleys and out towards the mountains are ample compensation for the quite steep climb up to the pasturelands of Untere Schneidalm on the sunny south-facing slopes above Pfelders. If you are not feeling energetic, try nearby Walk 24 instead!

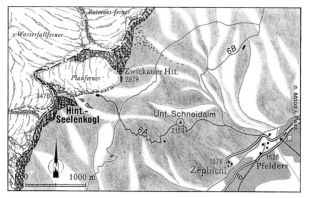

From Pfelders to the Untere Schneidalm □

From the bridge over the Pfelderer Stream follow the footpath (Route 6A) to the right. At a fork, bear left and zig-zag up the steep slopes. You will cross four streams before reaching the pastureland, Untere Schneidalm. The shelter lies a bit off the path; it's signposted.

The return □ Follow the same route back.

Variation for experienced mountain hikers □

From the Untere Schneidalm Route 6A continues to zig-zag up to the pastures of Obere Schneid, on very steep slopes with abrupt drops straight down to the Pfelderertal. If you continue up, you will come to the snowline, lying to the south of the ridge where the little Zwickauer Shelter is perched. Cross snow to the shelter. Reckon on two hours from the Untere Schneidalm to the Zwickauer Shelter. The high-level Pfelderer Höhenweg runs from here to the Stettinger Shelter — see Walks 7 and 21 (map page 25). This route has recently been repaired and waymarked. But even in summer the snow up here will be iced-over, and crampons are required. There is also some danger of rockfalls.

Opposite: the steep climb to the Untere Schneidalm

Approach: Bozen (262m/860ft), the capital city of the Bozen—Bolzano Province and the administrative and business centre of German-speaking South Tyrol. It's located at the confluence of the Etsch and Eisack valleys.

Starting point/parking: Klobenstein (1156m), seat of the Ritten municipality. You can get there by car, by bus from Bozen, or by tram and the connecting Ritterbahn via Oberbozen. Good parking in Klobenstein

Refreshments en route: There are several guesthouses and restaurants in Klobenstein and Lengmoos.

Walking time: from Klobenstein to the earthen pyramids about 1h; return 1h; *total walk 2h*

Grade: very easy ramble on a high mountain road

Best time of year: a good walk all year round, perhaps at its best in autumn

The Dolomites are mountains for the summer, for the sunshine months, when we are full of energy. But there are times when one would like to admire them from a distance. One of the best outlook balconies is the Ritten, a mountain on the western side of the Eisack Valley and the southernmost outpost of the Sarntal Alps. It's a peak just on your doorstep, if you are staying in Bozen — and easily accessible by bus, tram or car. So treat yourself to a relaxing

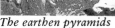
The earthen pyramids

day of photography and natural history when you visit Bozen: do the 'Fenn Ramble', an easy walk to the world-famous earthen pyramids. On the way you will see the picturesque church of St Nicholas at Mittelberg, set against the grandiose backdrop of the Schlern (Walks 28 and 29) and the Langkofel Group.

From Klobenstein via Lengmoos to the Ritten earthen pyramids □

From the centre of Klobenstein head for Lengmoos by road. At the end of Klobenstein, turn right onto the blue-and-white-signposted 'Fennpromenade' (Route 20). After passing through woods, you will make a wide arc to the left around the Fenn mountain. Here there are unimpeded views towards the peaks of the western Dolomites. From Lengmoos, follow the road towards Mittelberg, on the eastern slopes of the Ritten. On reaching a fork, bear right on Route 24 (1km from Lengmoos). You head for the Finsterbach gulley and come to a lookout platform with fine views over the pyramids.

Return □

Return the same way, or take the asphalt road from Lengmoos (shorter, but not so lovely).

Opposite: the Langkofel Group and the Schlern Massif, seen from the west

Nearest village: Tiers (1014m/3325ft), a summer resort in the inner Tierser Valley, easily reached by car or by bus from Bozen

Approach: Tiers (1014m/3325ft), a summer resort in the inner Tiers Valley, easily reached by car or by bus from Bozen

Refreshments en route: Tschamin Dairy Farm (1175m); there is a restaurant here, and they can accommodate overnight guests in the summer months.

Walking time: from Weißlahnbad up the Tschamintal to the Rechter Leger about 1h15min; the return about 45min; *total time under 2h*

Grade: an undemanding walk on well-signposted tracks and forestry roads

Highest point: Rechter Leger (1600m/5250ft), reached after a *climb of 433m/1420ft*

Best time of year: middle of May until the beginning of November

---

A 'perfect' valley — that's how one might describe the Tschamintal, nestled in the western side of the Rosengarten Group. Not only is it an archetypal Dolomite valley, but one of the most beautiful in the southern Alps. Midway up the Tschamin, the solitary splendour of the setting is especially breath-taking: here the

views towards the mighty towers of the Grasleiten and Valbona mountains (see opposite) are at their best.

From Weißlahnbad through the Tschamintal to the Rechter Leger □

Take the asphalt road and head northeast to the fork, where there's a signpost. Go straight on to a parking area, then down to the Tschaminbach. Cross the stream and continue to the dairy farm (Tschaminschwaige). From here a trail (Route 3, later Route 585) takes you across meadows and to the crossing of a forestry road. Go left on the forestry road; this leads you into a wide arc, and you round the right-hand side of the valley. Zigzag up to a crucifix (where there is a bench) and then to a fork. Here go straight ahead (east) on the cart-track; you cross to the left-hand side of the valley. Walking beside the stream, you climb to a woodland glade called the 'Erster Leger' ('First Floor'). Continue from here through a lovely wood, first on a level track and later more steeply uphill, to the extensive pastureland of the 'Rechter' ('Right-hand') Leger.

The descent □ To return, follow the same route.

Opposite: The towering peaks of the Grasleiten and Valbona ranges pierce the heavens above the Rechter Leger, a woodland glade where you will find some very picturesque cottages, tables and benches, and a beautifully-carved crucifix.

Approach: Völs (880m/2885ft), a holiday centre high above the Eisack Valley, on the western slopes of the Schlern; easily reached by car or by bus from Bozen

Starting point/parking: Völs

Refreshments en route: Völser Weiher Guesthouse (private, open year-round, 6 beds), or the Pension Waldsee (private, open year-round, 36 beds)

Walking time: Völs to the pond about 1h; from the pond to St Anton and back to Völs about 45min; *total time 1h45min*

Grade: easy circular walk

Highest point: Völser Weiher, a pond at 1036m/3400ft, reached after a *climb of 156m/510ft*

Best time of year: at its loveliest in early spring and autumn

Hint: If you are full of energy, why not continue from the pond to the Tuffalm? Just follow the waymarked lane from the Völser Weiher. It climbs east − towards the Schlern − through a Scots pine wood and up to the Tuff pasturelands, from where there is a very fine outlook over the sub-alpine mountains around Völs. This further climb is about 230m/755ft.

Balcony-like, terraced pasturelands high above Völs are the goal of this lovely circuit, which takes us high over the Eisacktal to the western outcrops of the Schlern. The Völser Weiher (Pond) is a little swimming spot set in a forest − and a very popular excursion point for groups of ramblers. The picturesque pond was originally created by the burghers of

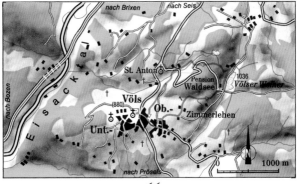

66

Völs, with the Schlern in the background

Völs-Colonna for carp-farming. If you want to enjoy this park-like setting at its finest, then you really should do the walk in the autumn, when the deep green colouring of the meadowlands provides the perfect foil for the rich red foliage.

From Völs via the Zimmerlehenhof to the pond □
Take the road southeast from Völs and climb up to the settlement of Obervöls. In the hamlet, bear left − northwest − on Route 1. You cross fields and reach the Hof Zimmerlehen, from where the route continues through woods up to the pond.

From the pond back to Völs, via St Anton □
First make for the Völser Weiher Guesthouse at the north end of the pond. From there head left, westwards, on Route 2. The first part of the way is on even ground, through woods. A gentle descent follows, and the settlement of St Anton is reached. From here, turn left onto a lane (before reaching the main road), to return to Völs.

Approach: Seis (997m/3270ft), a beautifully-situated health resort below the northern slopes of the Schlern

Parking/funicular: Park at the Frommer Guesthouse on the Seiser Alm toll road (4km from Seis). From here you can take the chair lift up to the Spitzbühel.

Starting point: Spitzbühel chair lift station (1935m), on the western edge of the Seiser Alm

Refreshments en route: Frommer Guesthouse (1720m, private, open year-round, 18 beds); Saltner Shelter (1731m, private, open from the beginning of June until the end of October, 8 beds); or the Schlernhaus (2457m, run by the Bozen branch of the Italian Alpine Club, open from 10 June until 5 October, 30 beds, 55 bunks)

Walking time: from the Spitzbühel to the Petz Peak on Schlern between 3h and 3h30min; return about 2h to 2h30min; *total time some 5-6 hours*

Grade: a fairly strenuous climb on very good tracks

Highest point: Mt Petz (2563m/8405ft), reached after a *climb of 628m/2060ft.* (Further climb of 105m en route)

Best time of year: early July until the end of September

Hint: An overnight stay at the Schlernhaus is highly recommended. You can watch the sun set and rise again over the Rosengarten and Latemar mountains

---

The Schlern, a colossal mass of rock that rears up out of the Eisack Valley on the western edge of the Dolomites, is a very popular excursion point for hikers. You can reach the 'Schlernhaus', the shelter run by the Italian Alpine Club, via many different routes. The mightiest upthrust from the Schlern Range is Mt

Looking southeast towards the Rosengarten range, from the 'Schlernhaus'. Try to spend the night here!

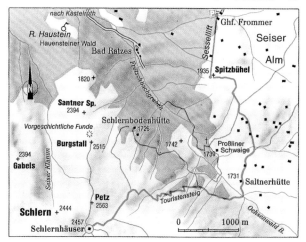

Petz, from where there are magnificent views towards other mountains in the Dolomites and the central and southern Urgestein Alps. From this summit there is also an unforgettable panorama over Völs, Seis and Kaselruth, deep in the valley below. The route to Mt Petz described here has been chosen because it is not unduly strenuous — thanks to the well-signposted, much-frequented tracks.

From the Spitzbühel chair lift station to the Schlernhaus □

Follow the track (Route 5) on the left-hand side of the Frötschbach gulley, crossing the pastures of the Tschapitalm in a southerly direction. It's a gentle climb as far as the Saltner Shelter. From there zig-zag steeply up southwest through dwarf-pines, climbing the slopes of Mt Petz. Once you are on the plateau-like eastern flanks of the mountain, head right, rounding the south side and then continuing west, gently uphill, to the Schlernhaus.

From the Schlernhaus to Mt Petz □

The way is well signposted and heads north over sometimes grassy land to the peak.

The descent □ To return, follow the same route.

Approach: St Ulrich (1236m/4055ft), a year-round sports centre midway up the Gröden Valley

Parking/funicular: Park at the Seiser Alm funicular station in St Ulrich. A cabin lift takes you up to the northern edge of the Seiser Alm.

Starting point: the guesthouse at the upper end of the cabin lift (2005m)

Refreshments en route: guesthouse at the top of the cabin lift (2005m, private, open from the beginning of May until the end of October, 20 beds); the Ikarus Guesthouse (1910m, private, open from 10 June until 15 October, 30 beds); or

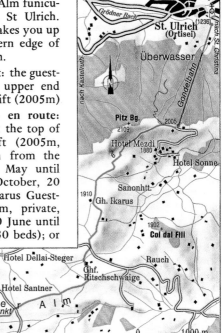

the Panorama Guesthouse (2011m, private, open all year round, 40 beds)

Walking time: from the guesthouse at the cabin lift to the Panorama Guesthouse about 1h15min–1h30min; return from the Panorama Guesthouse to the lift about 1h–1h15min; *total time under 2h45min*

Grade: an easy walk over pastureland

Highest point: Panorama Guesthouse, located at the saddle (2011m/6595ft). *Total climb throughout the walk about 140m/460ft*

Best time of year: a good all-year-round walk, perhaps at its best in early summer or autumn

---

Seiser Alm is Europe's largest alpine pastureland; surrounded by the massive peaks of the Dolomites, it is without doubt one of the most beautiful areas in the world for walking.

The possibilities for strolls and hikes are almost endless, and you can spend the whole day criss-crossing the pastures, forever discovering something new. So, even though the walk described here is quite short, be sure to allow plenty of time to do some exploring!

From the guesthouse at the top of the cabin lift to the Panorama Guesthouse □
Follow Route 6, making for the Pitzberg; you'll be walking westwards and will climb to a fork. Go left along the southern slopes of the mountain and through a light stand of stone-pines. The pines give way to open pastures, and you descend to the Ikarus Guesthouse. From here head south to the asphalt road. Follow it left towards the Ritschschwaige Guesthouse, but turn off right (signposted) before you get there. Then follow the (poorly-marked) Routes 6 and 10 southwest: you head uphill to a cart-track and follow it west to the crossing of an unsurfaced road. Continue straight over this road and now, on a lane, carry on to the Panorama Guesthouse at the saddle/viewing point.

Return □ Follow the same route back.

Looking west from the Seiser Alm towards Schlern and the Ortler Group

Approach: St Ulrich (1236m/4055ft), a year-round sports centre midway up the Gröden Valley

Parking/funicular: Park in St Ulrich and take the Raschötz chair lift.

Starting point: Raschötz chair lift station and restaurant (2107m)

Refreshments en route: Raschötz Shelter (2165m), run by the Italian Alpine Club and open from 20 May until the end of October (5 beds, 25 bunks)

Walking time: restaurant to the shelter about 20min; shelter to the Außerraschötz 30min; Außerraschötz to the Heiligkreuz Chapel and back down to the shelter and restaurant 1h; *total time under 2h*

Grade: an undemanding walk on good trails. Take care if it's misty around the Außerraschötz peak, however: there is a very steep drop on the north side!

Highest point: Außerraschötz (2281m/7480ft); this is reached after an *easy climb of 174m/570ft.*

Best time of year: beginning of June until the middle of October

Hint: It's easy to walk from the shelter back down to St Ulrich (about 1h30min−1h45min).

T hose 'in the know' regard the wide quartz-porphry summit of the Raschötz as the best viewing point in the Gröden Valley. Go and see for yourself! It's so easy to get there: just take the chair lift from St Ulrich up to the plateau and then follow the scenic upland track to the CAI (Club Alpino Italiano) Shelter. This is an unforgettable walk, with superb views over to the Sella Massif and the Langkofel Group opposite. From the summit of the nearby Außerraschötz the panorama opens out to embrace the surrounding western

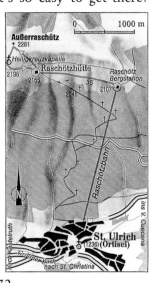

Looking southeast from the shelter at the Raschötz, there are superb views over the Sella, Marmolada and Langkofel peaks

Dolomites. You look out towards the Brenta, Adamello, Presanella and Ortler ranges, as well as the Ötztal, Stubai and Zillertal Alps.

From the chair lift/restaurant to the Raschötz Shelter □

Follow Route 35 westwards; it's well signposted. You'll pass through a light stand of stone-pines and then, climbing very gently, cross open alpine grazing land, following the southern flanks of the Raschötz ridge.

Circuit from the shelter to the Außerraschötz and the Holy Cross Chapel; return to St Ulrich □

Take Route 35 northwest over the stony pasturelands up to the summit, where there is a cross. Then go over the southwestern ridge and on to the chapel below. Here keep left on Route 35 to follow the southern flanks of the mountain eastwards, back to the shelter. Return to St Ulrich by chair lift or on foot.

Approach: St Peter in Villnöß (1154m/3785ft), the largest village in the Villnöß Valley, accessible by car or bus from Klausen or Brixen

Starting point/parking: Ranui (1346m), a farm at the entrance to the Villnöß Valley: Go straight ahead on a lane (closed to through traffic), where the main asphalt road swings left into the Zannser Valley. The charming little church of St Johann is nearby.

Refreshments en route: Brogles Shelter (2045m, open from 20 June to 3 October, 20 beds)

Walking time: from Ranui Farm to the Broglesalm about 2h; return about 1h15min; *total time 3h15min*

Grade: a fairly strenuous, but not difficult, climb on good tracks or forestry roads

Highest point: Broglesalm (2045m/6705ft), reached after a *climb of 699m/2295ft*

Best time of year: beginning of July until the end of October

Hint: Be sure to continue from the shelter to the Brogles Scharte, a gap 15 minutes further on, from where there are wonderful views towards Schlern in the southwest.

This walk takes us up to the lofty heights of the inner Villnöß Valley, where sleepy alpine pastures lie at the foot of the jagged Geisler peaks. To get there, reckon on a stiff

climb. But once you
reach the shelter, the
heavens open up and
what a view! When
you see the mighty
northern walls of the
Geisler and Fermeda
peaks towering above,
you'll forget the tiring
ascent. Take a break
here, and daydream,
while you contem-
plate the play of light
and shade on this
magnificent   alpine
tableau.

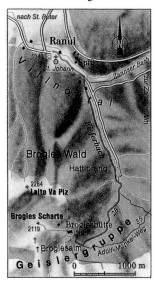

From the Ranui Farmstead in the Villnößtal to the Broglesalm □

We follow the forestry road (closed to through traffic) southeast, climbing ever higher in the Villnöß Valley. At the fork, bear right to follow the route up the Klieferbachtal, heading almost due south. When the road ends, continue on the good trail (Route 28), climbing steadily in bends up through the forest. A fork is met: keep right (southwest) and pass a waterfall. Soon we are out of the forest and, still climbing, we meet the crossing of the Adolf-Munkel-Weg (Route 35). Turn right to cross a basin and make for the Broglesalm and shelter. After taking a break here for a picnic lunch, be sure to walk west to the Brogles Scharte ('Brogles Gap', fifteen minutes away), to enjoy the fine views towards the Schlern (Walk 29) in the southwest.

The return □ To descend follow the same route.

Opposite: The blissfully peaceful Broglesalm, below the jagged peaks of the Geisler Range (seen from the west)

Approach: St Ulrich (1236m/4055ft), a year-round sports and holiday centre located midway up the Gröden Valley

Starting point/parking: square in front of the parish church in St Ulrich

Refreshments en route: Jakoberhof Hotel in the hamlet of St Jakob (1433m)

Walking time: from St Ulrich to the Col de Flam and on to the church of St Jakob about 45min; from the church to the hamlet of St Jakob and back to St Ulrich about 30min—45min; *total time under 1h30min*

Grade: an easy circular walk on good tracks or roads

Hightest point: St Jakob Church (1565m/5135ft), reached after a *climb of 329m/1080ft*

Best time of year: possible all year round, but at its loveliest in early spring when the wild flowers are out — or in autumn, when the colours are changing

---

St Jakob, the oldest church in the Gröden Valley (13th century), contains a number of marvellous frescoes. It's another well-known mecca for walkers in the Dolomites, and the impressive landscape appeals to photographers especially. The church stands on open ground facing the Langkofel, a peak that looks from here like a hand reaching up to the heavens. The setting is totally peaceful — a perfect place to tarry and to contemplate. This little mountain

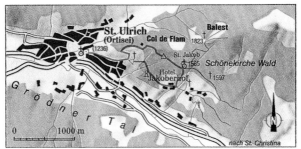

church is the focal point of an easy circular walk from St Ulrich. All along the way you'll enjoy marvellous views of the mountains surrounding the inner Gröden Valley.

From St Ulrich to the Col de Flam and the mountain church of St Jakob □

From the parish church, start out by taking the asphalt road heading east uphill towards the hamlet of St Jacob (Routes 4 and 6). Then turn left on a signposted lane, to climb in a northerly direction to the lower slopes on the southwestern side of the Pitschberg. Crossing the Col de Flam, bear right to a chapel with a very large crucifix and then go through a beautiful larch forest and over pastureland, from where you'll have splendid views of the Langkofel. Continue uphill to a saddle and crossroads: here go right and follow the southern flanks of the Pitschberg. You'll head east through a Scots pine wood and -- still slightly climbing – come to the idyllic setting of St Jakob (shown opposite).

From the church to the hamlet and St Ulrich □

From the church follow Route 6 (signposted), heading southeast initially and then south (right) over pastures. Descend to the road and bear right to St Jakob (1433m). The return route to St Ulrich follows the asphalt road, through forests and amidst grazing land; it's a gentle descent.

Opposite: St Jakob's magnificent setting, looking out to the upstretched 'hand' of the Langkofel

Approach: Kolfuschg (1615m/5295ft), a well-known holiday centre with good views towards the Sella Group

Parking/funicular: Park in the centre of Kolfuschg. A short climb takes you to the chair lift station; from there take the chair lift to the Col Pradat.

Starting point: Col Pradat Shelter (2036m), at the end of the chair lift

Refreshments en route: Col Pradat Shelter (2036m), open all year round

Walking time: from the shelter to Lake Champai ('Campaccio-See' on the map) about 45min; return about 30min; *total time about 1h15min*

Grade: easy

Highest point: Lake Chiampai (2173m/7125ft), reached after an *easy climb of 137m/450ft*

Best time of year: late June until the end of September

Hints: From the lake, you can continue uphill another 193m/635ft (follow Route 4) to the Chiampaijoch, a saddle from where there are splendid views to the Pelmo and Civetta peaks. On the return journey, rather than take the chair lift, why not walk back down to Kolfuschg through the Stella Alpina Valley — this takes only 30min at most.

---

*E*nchantingly beautiful, the area around the Chiampai Lake is another favourite excursion point for walkers. The small lake sits in a depression in the upper Stella Alpina Valley above the Ladin village of Kolfuschg. The easiest

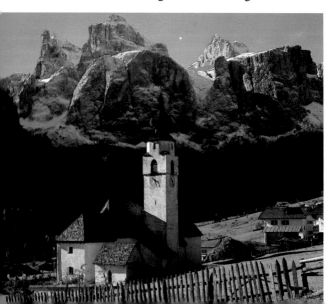

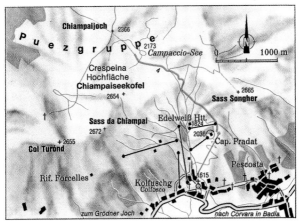

way to get there is to take the chair lift up over the valley to the Col Pradat. Not only will you see the lovely lake, but on the way you will enjoy marvellous views towards the southeastern Dolomites.

From the Col Pradat Shelter to the lake □
Take the well-signposted track beneath the southwestern inclines of the Sass Songher. Head northwest on the almost-even track, and you'll reach a very picturesque chapel. Come to the crossing of Route 4 and head right to climb the valley lying between the Sass da Chiampai and the Sass Songher. Another mountain crossroads is met: here Route 7 branches off right to the Sass Songher. Keep straight ahead (west) on Route 4. A short climb takes you from here to the lovely lake, set in a pebbly basin.

The descent □ Follow the same route to return.

Kolfuschg, with the Sella Group in the background

Approach: Corvara (1555m/5100ft), an important holiday area in the Ladin-speaking Gader Valley

Parking/funicular: Park in Corvara, at the station for the Crep de Mont cabin lift. Take this lift to the Crep de Mont station; from there take the Vallonkar lift.

Starting point: Vallon chair lift station (2553m)

Refreshments en route: Crep de Mont (2152m, open summer and winter), Hotel Boè (1860m, private, open from the beginning of July until mid-September)

Walking time: from the Vallon station at the upper end of the chair lift to the Col de Stagn 15min; from there back to Crep de Mont and the Campolungo Pass (a descent) about 1h–1h15min; *total time under 1h30min*

Grade: an easy descent on well-built and well-signposted paths. You must, however, be sure-footed and have a head for heights.

Highest point: top end of the Vallon chair lift (2553m/ 8375ft). This is reached by the double chair lift. From here there is a *descent of 693m/2275ft.*

Best time of year: beginning of July until the end of September

Here's a perfect example of the 'downhill mountain-climbing' referred to in the Foreword! Up on the east side of the Sella Group, from the Col de Stagn on the edge of the mighty Vallonkar, you will overlook a great part of the eastern Dolomites — from the Heiligkreuz-kofel on the left all the way round via Tofana, Pelmo and Civetta, to Marmolada on the right.

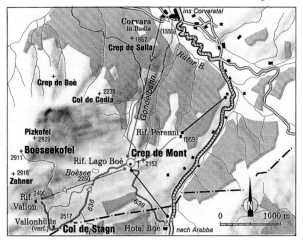

Having reached the highest point in the walk by lift, you can now look forward to a leisurely downhill stroll and a bus or taxi ride from the Campolungo Pass back to Corvara.

From the top end of the Vallon chair lift to the Col de Stagn □
Go south on the signposted route into a basin and then to a fork, where there is another sign-post. Now it's just a short climb up to the top of the Col de Stagn and the wonderful panorama.

Descent to the Hotel Boè via Crep de Mont □
More signposting leads you downhill north into another basin and to another fork. Here bear right (northeast) on Route 636. You will zig-zag down steep, stony pastureland slopes and pass under the chair lift. The Boè Lake sits below a rock wall on your left. A short walk to the east brings you to the top end of the Crep de Mont cabin lift. From here follow the unsurfaced road (Route 638) to the right, to cross meadows and descend to the Campolungo road, which is met near the Hotel Boè (some 500m/yds north of the Campolungo Pass). From the hotel take a bus or taxi to Corvara.

Opposite: Views to Marmolada from the Vallonkar

Approach: St Vigil (1193m/3195ft), a holiday centre at the entrance to the Rautal

Starting point/parking: Pederü Guesthouse (1545m), at the end of the Rautal, reached from St Vigil by bus or car (12 parking places)

Overnight suggestion: Pederü Guesthouse (1540m, private, open from 1 June to 20 October, 25 beds); Fanes Shelter (2060m, private, open from the beginning of June until the end of September, 35 beds, 32 bunks); or La Varella Shelter (2042m, private, open from the beginning of June until the end of September, 27 beds, 8 bunks)

Walking time: from the Pederü Guesthouse to the Fanes Shelter about 1h30min—2h; the return about 1h—1h15min; *total time about 3h*

Grade: quite an easy climb along good tracks

Highest point: the Fanes Shelter (2060m/6755ft), reached after a *climb of 515m/1690ft*

Best time of year: beginning of June until the end of October

Hints: There is a regular jeep service between the Pederü Guesthouse and the Fanes Shelter. If you take it to the Fanes Shelter, you can simply walk downhill. From the Fanes Shelter you can also walk to the Grünsee (2042m), the Limosee (2159m), or to Große Fanesalm (2104m); these are all short excursions signposted in the area and taking between 30min and 1h30min return.

Gasthof Pederü, situated at the top end of the Rautal, is the focal point for several walks to the high-lying pastures of Fanes and Sennes and their upland shelters. One of the loveliest excursions is the one described here: it visits Kleine Fanesalm — the 'Little Pastureland' of Fanes. It must be admitted that the

The Grünsee, a small lake near the Fanes Shelter

fairly monotonous walk along the track is not particularly interesting, but once you reach the upper meadows, a wonderful Dolomite landscape reveals itself in all its majesty: endless expanses, closely-knit upthrusts of rock, massive screes, rock layers exposed like the facets of a precious gem, and a multitude of jagged peaks and towers.

The juxtaposition of this wonderland of rock and the tiny lakes and meadows scattered below results in a somewhat unreal, fairytale-like landscape.

From the Pederü Guesthouse to Kleine Fanesalm and return □

Follow the track (Route 7) south through the Vallon di Rudo. At first the going is on level ground, but then the way zig-zags steeply up to the middle of the valley and the Pischadèl Lake. From here we head west through an uninteresting landscape of grazing ground and dwarf pines. Crossing the Vigilbach and bearing south, we reach the Kleine Fanesalm, where there are two shelters, Fanes (left) and La Varella (right).

The return □ Follow the same route to descend.

Approach: Niederdorf (1154m/3785ft), or Welsberg (1087m/3565ft), international holiday centres in the upper Pustertal

Starting point/parking: Hotel Pragser Wildsee (1494m), accessible by bus from the Niederdorf bus station or by car from Niederdorf or Welsberg (11km)

Refreshments en route: Hotel Pragser Wildsee (1494m, private, open from May until September, 220 beds)

Walking time: *total time for the circuit 1h*

Grade: an easy walk; there are fences along exposed stretches.

Best time of year: mid-May until October. Best light in high summer. Note that on weekends it will be very crowded here!

The Pragser Wildsee is an exceptionally beautiful lake set in a secluded basin on the edge of the Dolomites. And the surrounding landscape is superb: The 1000m-high northern wall of the Seekofel, the mighty Roßkofel and the Herrstein form an austere massif — a backdrop more reminiscent of the northern Calcareous Alps than the 'youthful Dolomites'. A large hotel stands on the northern banks of this legendary lake; it's easily reached by car via a

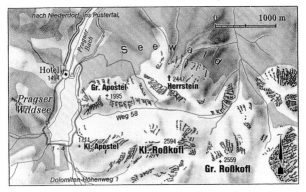

good asphalt road. Many excursions are possible from this base — both short rambles and several long hikes and climbs in the Prags and Enneberg Dolomites.

Around the Pragser Wildsee □

From the hotel head south on Route 1 (part of the Dolomites 'High-Level Route' 1). You make your way into the valley and, near the south-western corner of the lake, you come to a fork. Here go left on Route 1—4, to head east along the bank. In a few minutes come to another fork; here the Dolomite 'Höhenweg' 1 bears right (signposted). We go left, to follow the eastern banks of the lake below the fringes of the 'Little' (Kl.) and 'Big' (Gr.) Apostels. At some points the path has been blasted from the rock and is exposed; there is very adequate fencing, however. On coming to the most northerly tip of the lake, Route 58 comes in to join us. We follow this to the left to return to the hotel.

Opposite: the emerald beauty of the Pragser Wildsee

Approach: Niederdorf (1154m/3785ft), an international tourist centre in the upper Pustertal, or Schluderbach (1438m/4715ft), a grouping of hotels in the heart of the Höhlensteintal

Starting point/parking: Plätzwiese (2000m), a pastureland saddle between the Dürrenstein in the east and the Hohe Gaisl in the west. Park at the Hotel Plätzwiese at the pass, or south of the pass — at the Hotel Hohe Gaisl or the Dürrenstein Shelter. The area is accessible by car only (14km from Niederdorf, 7km from Schluderbach)

Refreshments en route: Gasthof Plätzwiese (1991m, private, open all year round), Hotel Hohe Gaisl (1991m, private, open all year round except November, 64 beds), Dürrenstein Shelter (2040m, private, open all year round, 16 beds, 16 bunks)

Walking time: from the Dürrenstein Shelter to the Strudelköpfe between 45min and 1h; the descent about 45min; *total time 1h30min−1h45min*

Grade: an easy climb on an old military road (sometimes waymarked). Take care at the top of the Strudelköpfe if it's misty!

Highest point: Strudelköpfe (2308m/7570ft), reached after a *climb of 268m/880ft* (from the Dürrenstein Shelter)

Best time of year: beginning of June until the end of October

O ne of the most magical settings in the northern Dolomites is the area around the Plätzwiese Pass, where the overnight accommodation is also excellent. Many come here to climb the Dürrenstein (2839m), known for its magnificent views. But for walkers more modest in their appetites, the Strudelköpfe Peak in the southeast is more easily tackled, and the views from there down into the heart of the Höhlen-

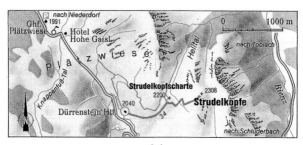

Looking south towards the Cristallo Group from the Plätzwiese

stein Valley are superb. On a day when clouds are skudding across the sky, the play of light and shade on the magnificent massif of the Sexten Dolomites and the Cadin and Cristallo groups is simply fantastic.

From the Dürrenstein Shelter to the Strudel-köpfe □
Take Route 34 and head east into a deep gulley. Follow the left-hand side of the gulley to zig-zag up to the gentle meadowlands west of the peak. Here go straight ahead through a basin to the broad Strudelkopf Gap (2200m), where there are the remains of old military fortifications. Now head southeast on the old military road to curl your way uphill, later turning left. When the road fades out, continue in an easterly direction (on no particular path), to cross the pastureland and come to the highest point on the mountain (2308m).

The descent □ Follow the same route to return.

Approach: Cortina d'Ampezzo (1211m/3970ft), a popular tourist centre in the upper Boite Valley, or Schluderbach (1438m/4715m), a grouping of hotels in the heart of the Höhlensteintal

Starting point/parking: Angelo Bosi Shelter (2205m), on the southeastern edge of the Piana Plateau. Reach it by car either from Cortina (21km) or from Schluderbach (13km). Go via Misurina; the narrow Monte Piana road is north of the lake.

Refreshments en route: Angelo Bosi Shelter (2205m, private, open from mid-May until the end of October, 20 beds, 11 bunks).

Walking time: *total time to round the peak 2—3h*

Grade: You must be sure-footed and have a head for heights. The paths are well protected, however.

Highest point: Mount Piana's southernmost peak (2324m/7620ft). *Total climb on the walk about 220m/720ft*

Best time of year: beginning of June until the end of October

A hefty wedge between the Rienza and Popena valleys, Monte Piana is an excellent lookout point. Up on the summit, you are at the same height as the enormous massif of the eastern Dolomites — and at just the right distance to appreciate their force and mass. Countless old dugouts, left-over barbed wire, and the remains of barracks are reminders of the importance of Monte Piana during the War in the Dolomites (1915-18), when the (higher) southern peak was in the hands of the Italians and the northern peak under the control of Austria. A recently-opened outdoor museum lies en route between the two peaks; you'll see it on this circular walk.

88

Circuit around Monte Piana □

From the Angelo Bosi Shelter take Route 122 and head northwest up to the Piana plateau. Continue over wavy ground, rutted by numerous gulleys. On coming to the southern peak (the highest, at 2324m), you will find a memorial to the poet Carducci. From here go downhill north to the saddle, the Forcella di Val dei Castrati, where there is a fork. Keep right here, on the eastern side of the mountain, and you will come across the old military remains. Carry on to the northern peak (2320m), marked by a a cross. From there continue downhill in a southerly direction, to return to the Castrati Saddle. Then, keeping the southern peak on your right, walk back southeast to the Angelo Bosi Shelter (Route 6a).

Monte Piana and the little chapel in front of the Angelo Bosi Shelter

Approach: Innichen (1173m/3845ft), a market town on the north edge of the Dolomites, in the upper Pustertal

Starting point/parking: Lanzinger Säge (1259m), a group of houses at the mouth of the Innerfeldtal in the Sexten Valley, reached by car or by bus from Innichen

Refreshments en route: the Dreischuster Shelter (1626m, run by the Sexten Alpine Club, open from 1 June until 30 September, 40 beds, 20 bunks)

Walking time: Lanziger Säge to the Dreischuster Shelter about 1h30min; return 1h15min; *total time 2h45min*

Grade: an easy climb, sometimes on roads

Highest point: the Dreischuster Shelter (1626m/5335ft), reached after a *climb of 358m/1175ft*

Best time of year: middle of May until the end of October

Hint: You can also park 4km beyond Lanziger Säge at the Antoninstein (where there is a road barrier) and walk from there to the shelter in 30min.

While the mountains of the Innerfeldtal cannot compare in majesty with those of the nearby Fischleintal (Walk 41), whoever comes to this little-visited side-valley will find that its beauty is second to none in the Sexten Dolomites. This walk takes us from Lanzinger

Säge in the Sextental to the Dreischuster Shelter on the upper reaches of the Innerfeldtal, and throughout the walk we are accompanied by fascinating views over towards the proud rock-pinnacles of the Haunold and Dreischuster peaks.

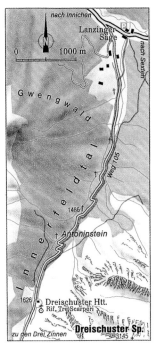

From Lanziger Säge to the Dreischuster Shelter □ Take the grassy track heading uphill south to the narrow lane. Follow this lane into the valley, through lovely stands of larch trees. You come to a large parking area at the Antoninstein. Just beyond this, the road bends to follow the left-hand side of the valley. From here we can take a short-cut (waymarked in red, Route 105) up through a light wood and then dwarf pines; it takes us back up to the road, from where it's an easy walk to the shelter. On the way there are very fine views of the rocky massif of the Morgenkopf at the upper end of the valley. When the upper meadowlands are reached, turn left to the shelter, which stands in a light spruce wood.

The return walk □ Follow the same route back.

Opposite: approaching the Dreischuster Shelter from the Innerfeldtal, with the rocky mass of the Morgenkopf rising in the background

Approach: Sexten (1316m/4315ft), one of the best-known tourist centres in the South Tyrol. The village is set in an off-shoot of the Pustertal.

Starting point/parking: Sexten (good parking)

Refreshments en route: Dolomitenhof Hotel (1454m, private, open year-round, 100 beds)

Walking time: from Sexten to the hotel (Fischleinboden) about 1h15min; the return about 1h–1h15min; *total time some 2h30min*

Grade: an easy walk on well-signposted tracks

Highest point: Dolomitenhof Hotel (1454m/4770ft), reached after a *climb of 137m/450ft*

Best time of year: beginning of May to the end of October, but at its best in early summer and autumn

Hint: If you have time and energy, you can walk from the hotel to the Talschluß shelter (1540m). This takes only 30min and affords wonderful views of the nearby Einserkofel (the 'First Summit')

One of the most beautiful and popular easy walks in the Dolomites, this route — a 'must' for anyone who loves the region — takes us from Sexten up to the Fischleinboden. The gorgeous Fischlein Valley with its enchanting larch-wooded meadows and views towards the upthrust pinnacles of the 'Sexten Sundial' are reason enough to do the walk — even if you

don't climb to the peaks or shelters. The walk described here ends about mid-way up the valley, at the Dolomitenhof Hotel. Along the way, you look out to the peaks called the 'Tenth, Eleventh, Twelfth and First' summits — see photograph page 94 and caption page 95.

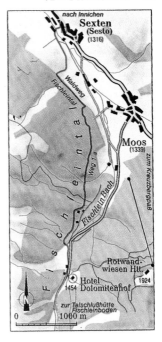

From Sexten to the Dolomitenhof Hotel at the Fischleinboden □

From the tourist office in the centre of town follow the Moos road for 100m (yards). Then turn right on a small asphalt lane (signposted), to cross the Sexten Stream and walk up to a crossroads. Bear left here on a fenced-off trail (Route 1a, 'Waldweg in das Fischleintal'). First you cross flat meadows, heading southeast; then the route heads right, uphill, to the treeline. The good trail carries you to an unsurfaced road, which you then follow south through forest to the (ruined) Heideck Fort. Now continue through the setting shown opposite, on the right-hand side of the valley. Soon an unsurfaced road is met; it takes you to the hotel.

Return □

You can either follow the same route back, or return to Sexten by bus from the hotel.

Opposite: the larch-proud meadows of the Fischleintal

Approach: Sexten (1316m/4315ft), one of the best-known tourist centres in the South Tyrol. The village is set in an off-shoot of the Pustertal.

Parking/funicular: Park at the Helm cabin lift station at the eastern entrance to Sexten. From there take the cabin lift to Helm.

Starting point: upper end of the cabin lift (2060m), on the western flanks of the Helm

Refreshments en route: restaurant at the cabin lift station (2060m), or the Panorama Guesthouse halfway up the mountain (1570m)

Walking time: from the top of the lift to Sexten: *2h total*

Grade: an easy descent on good roads

Highest point: top of the cabin lift (Mt Helm, 2060m/6755ft), from where there is a *descent of 743m/2435ft to Sexten*

Best time of year: middle of June until the beginning of October

Hint: From the top of the cabin lift you can easily climb to the summit of Helm, by following a military road and heading east past the Hahnspiel Shelter to the southern ridge. Crossing it, and following Route 4a to the left, you attain the summit in about 1h (2433m/7980ft).

---

*I*f you would like to admire the Dolomites from a distance rather than have more 'close-up' views, here's a walk that will give you a new perspective on the range. By cabin lift, you glide

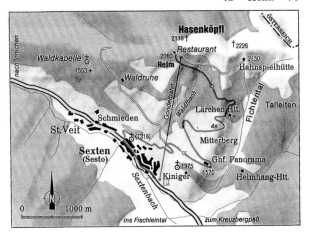

up the Helm, a mountain that towers over the northern side of Sexten and serves as a sort of 'boundary marker' for the western end of the Karnish Alps. The Helm is an excellent viewpoint, set between the glaciers of the central Alps to the north and the magnificent rock world of the Dolomites in the south. Thanks to the cabin lift, you can now wander downhill on one of the many tracks on the southern slopes of the mountain, through larch-wooded meadows, and with the 'Sexten Sundial' always in sight.

Descent from the cabin lift station to Sexten □
Follow the narrow road (Route 4a; closed to traffic) downhill, over bare pastureland and then through larch trees. Wide bends carry you to Mitterberg, where here is an old Austrian fort and the Panorama Guesthouse. From here there are also wonderful views to the Fischleintal opposite (Walk 41), with the 'hours' of the 'Sexten Sundial' in the background. A curving asphalt road takes you from Mitterberg back to Sexten.

Opposite: On our descent down the southern inclines of the Helm, there are especially good views towards the 'Sexten Sundial' (see Walk 41). The peaks in the photograph are called the 'Tenth, Eleventh, Twelfth and First' summits and are ranged as they would be on a clock.

Numbers following entries are *walk* numbers, *not* page numbers. For mountain groups, see Contents. Spellings below (whether German or Italian) correspond to those used for the *walk title and the walking maps*; in the text itself, many terms have been translated into English.